Commen

Kingdom life can be full of sto...... ...ne in the trenches of ministry can leave even the most dedicated of Christian workers with a weariness of the soul. Storms take their toll and all of us at times can feel like the disciples on that storm-tossed vessel on the Galilean seas, gasping with what might feel like our last breath: *"Master, do you not care that we are perishing?"*

Ellel Ministry came into our lives during a time when the ministry boat of the church family, which my wife and I have the great honor of leading, was in desperate need of a safe harbor. Intense relational strain, sudden leadership changes, core structural shifts and far-reaching cultural course corrections came together in a perfect storm that left us gasping for breath.

Derek and Beryl Puffett were instrumental in helping us make sense of it all. Through their faithful prayers, wise counsel, utmost confidentiality and above all, their example, they have demonstrated that it is possible to go through the highs and lows of ministry and personal life and still be filled with faith and excitement for the future. They have never given up on the local church and have inspired us to do the same.

This book which Derek has written does not come from the perspective of an outsider. Derek and Beryl love Jesus and they love His Bride. Nothing gives them greater joy than to see the Bride embrace healing, and nothing gives them greater pain than to see her suffer because she refuses to be healed or delivered.

Whether it was journeying on a personal level with Nikki and myself, or providing invaluable leadership insights into the relationships, structures and culture of our bigger Shofar Christian Church family, they have done so as people who partner with the Holy Spirit to come alongside the Bride, and to journey with her to where Father God wants her to be.

I am in no doubt that this book will help you navigate the storms of Kingdom life, whilst at the same time empowering you and pointing you to the Rock, Jesus Christ of Nazareth, who is the safest place of all.

Heinrich and Nikki Titus

International Team Leaders
Shofar Christian Church

Eyes Closed
Eyes Opened

'Open their eyes so that they
may turn from darkness to light'
Acts 26:18

Derek Puffett

First published June 2021

Distributor: Ellel Ministries South Africa
Email: bookshop@ellel.org
Website: https://ellel-shere.myshopify.com/
Tel: +27128091172/0031

Also available as an e-book   ISBN 978-0-620-94376-5

Cover design by Lené A Pienaar –info@leneartstudio.com

Printed in Great Britain by Bell & Bain Ltd, Glasgow

⁂ Dedication ⁂

Beryl my dearest wife
for fifty years and counting.

Your unfailing love is immeasurable. How would I have
managed life without you? Completing this book without
your encouragement would not have happened.

Love you Sweets!

To my family, my friends and my team at Ellel Shere
House, for their amazing support and who have spurred me
on.

To Peter and Fiona, thank you for your interest, inspiration
and guidance.

To Paul, Liz, Margie and Christel for your hours and hours
of guidance and input in this my first book.

Thank you Lené for offering your artistic talent for the front
and back covers.

*'But seek first his kingdom and his righteousness, and all
these things will be given to you as well.'*

(Matthew 6:33)

Table of Contents

Foreword

Life is pretty busy for me these days, and I don't have enough time to read all the good new books that cross my desk. They fall into three categories:

1. The books I won't ever have the time to read.
2. The books that join a pile by my bedside that I want to read sometime, and
3. The books I start reading right away and don't want to put down till they're finished!

Eyes Closed Eyes Opened is definitely in the third category. For that's exactly what happened to me when I started reading the manuscript!

I was gripped by the reality of Derek Puffett's journey of faith and his personal honesty, which will encourage the reader not to dismiss the very real message of this inspiring read.

Derek's love for the Church and its leaders pervades every page of the book. But so does his grief at how the Church so often fails to live in the reality of what Jesus intended the Church to be. His own experience of knocking on the doors of many churches, and asking fundamental questions about life and God, but not getting the answers he was so desperately looking for, have motivated the rest of his life.

He became determined to not only find the answers to his own questions, but to ensure that when he found them, he would do everything he could to tell others the good news. As a result, Derek is one of the most natural and effective personal evangelists I know. I have watched him in action, chatting to the waiter in a café or the person filling up his car with petrol, and been amazed at the fruit of his conversations.

But he is not only an evangelist to those who are outside the Kingdom of God, he is an evangelist to those inside the Church as well, spreading the reality of the life-transforming and healing message that Jesus came to bring.

This is an important book – it will be challenging and life-changing to those who grasp its message. I pray it will be read by many, especially leaders who, like Derek, are longing for the Church to actually be the Body of Christ taking God's healing into a broken and desperate world. Prepare to be surprised and blessed!

Peter Horrobin

Founder and International Director
Ellel Ministries
Ellel Grange, June 2021

Preface

Jesus commissioned the Apostle Paul in a dramatic way, and his call and commissioning were instantaneous. His response was just as dramatic, as the fear of the Lord was upon him, and from that incredible moment, when he knew it was Jesus speaking to him, he never once, even in the direst circumstances, wavered from his calling. In the same way, I believe the commissioning of a disciple today is just as much a call and a command from Jesus Himself. The commissioning is for every Christian and is intended to be used for Jesus' Church.

> *We all fell to the ground, and I heard a voice saying to me in Aramaic, 'Saul, Saul, why do you persecute me? It is hard for you to kick against the goads.' Then I asked, 'Who are you, Lord?' 'I am Jesus, whom you are persecuting,' the Lord replied. 'Now get up and stand on your feet. I have appeared to you to appoint you as a servant and as a witness of what you have seen of me and what I will show you. I will rescue you from your own people and from the Gentiles. I am sending you to them to open their eyes and turn them from darkness to light, and from the power of Satan to God, so that they may receive forgiveness of sins and a place among those who are sanctified by faith in me'. (Acts 26:14-18)*

How many times have I read this portion of Scripture? How many times have I listened to it and preached on it myself? But one day, while reading it, God spoke so directly to me it was scary. There and then I had to examine myself – and I was found wanting. Although these words were addressed to

Paul, they are also intended for His call upon the Church. It's stunning!

My objective in writing this book is not to make it theologically complicated and profound, but for it to be profound in its simplicity. My hope is that spiritual eyes will be opened to scriptures that are sometimes glossed over and made to sound unimportant. Yet, when allowed to touch our hearts, these scriptures are potentially life changing.

The Bible is not complicated. It was never intended to be. However, it does help for someone to come alongside and connect the dots, so we can see the relevance for our everyday lives. During the early years of my Christian walk it helped me so much when someone pointed out biblical aspects which opened my eyes to understanding meaning for my own life. And when I gained understanding, I could successfully effect change in my life. It's a matter of discipleship.

Often, we search for the lost, meaning those whose eyes are spiritually closed, and we open their eyes to Jesus. However, if we do not teach and apply the full Gospel, we effectively close their eyes to the physical, emotional, mental and spiritual healing Jesus has made available. It's a case of eyes closed, eyes opened, and then eyes closed, or partially closed, to God's truth.

I love the Church in its diversity. We can learn so much from one another. But let's face it, churches and church denominations have diverse opinions regarding salvation, discipleship, setting captives free from demonic oppression, the work of the Holy Spirit and discerning biblical truth. So, this book may challenge some of your theological thinking and the beliefs handed down to you by your family or church traditions.

When reading 'Eyes Closed Eyes Opened', will you ask the Holy Spirit to open your spiritual eyes to the truths in the teaching of Jesus? Every teaching of Jesus is intended for today. I encourage you to measure what you have been taught, or not taught, against what the Bible says, and have the courage to renew your mind in line with God's truth.

My vision is to see the Church of Jesus Christ become the effective Church Jesus intended her to be. It's all about the Kingdom of God. In a simple way, I guess, I am aiming to steady the boat through rough theological seas and navigate truths that will give direction to the Gospel in all its fullness. This cannot be achieved with spiritually closed or half-closed eyes. I believe Father God wants the Body of Christ to become more effective and true to her call to continue the work of Jesus here on earth.

Many of these truths are simply left out of the teaching programs of the Church, which robs God's people from being all that they could be. A disciple of Jesus is a follower of Jesus, one who walks in His footsteps, doing what He did, and continuing His work on earth, without doubt or deception. Unfortunately, many Christians are not taught about following Jesus in their God-given authority. The Church is not the building, but those who believe and have received Jesus as Lord and Savior of their life. They are the ones who should be equipped to follow Jesus, and, in His name, continue to do good works, the good works Jesus taught and demonstrated in the Gospels.

Jesus was the most effective and powerful person who ever lived. After His death, Luke, in the Book of the Acts of the Apostles, recorded the continuation of the same amazing ministry taught and so powerfully demonstrated by Jesus. As the Church grew, it quickly became a powerful force in communities around the world. God at work in His people needs to continue through His people even today. Jesus seemed to use a 'hear, see, and then do' type of training. They heard His message, they saw Him applying the Word, and then He sent them out to do the same. Taking away anything from what Jesus taught His disciples will divert from what He intended for His Church and will result in a Church which is irrelevant.

We may be able to create a wonderful family atmosphere, but if we are not continuing the works of Jesus, then we will become only a social and religious group. Is this what the Church of Jesus Christ is about? Jesus took every opportunity to demonstrate the authenticity of the power of God after preaching the Word. If I were asked, "What is the job description of the Church today?" I would answer, "To continue the work of Jesus on earth". Are our intentions leaning in that direction? It might be helpful to re-read the Book of Acts.

We need to bear in mind that a church with many members does not necessarily reflect the Church as God intended it to be. For instance, I believe many people have stopped seeking healing or answers to life from their church. What if we measured our church against the examples we have of the early Church in Acts?

Following Jesus in the early Church was never comfortable. So, if we are feeling comfortable today, despite today's hostile spiritual climate being much as it was in those days, could it be that we are not being truly effective in following Jesus? My heart, and the purpose of this book, is for us to get back to the simple basics of who we believe Jesus is and who *we* are in Christ.

To achieve this, each one of us needs to look at our personal lives and measure them against the plumb line of the life of our Savior. We will probably find we are so 'out of line' with our Savior that it may shock us. Many Christians need discipleship training which enables them to confidently receive healing in a safe environment. For once we have received healing, we can make our lives right with God and can start to do the same works as Jesus.

This was the position I found myself in. I was so unhealed and in various forms of bondage that I could never live the life of freedom that Jesus and His disciples spoke of. Even after coming to the reality of who I was in Christ Jesus and after being a pastor for twelve years, I knew I fell far short of where I should have been. I was determined to make right with God, whatever it might cost in pride and humility to get there.

I'm so glad I made that decision to face reality and the consequences. I was fortunate to have met up with some people from Ellel Ministries who understand and respect hurting people and those looking for a safe place to make right with God. Looking back over my life in Christ, the opportunity to deal with the unwanted stuff in my life should have been available soon after my conversion to Jesus. It would have helped so much.

Some people are utterly determined to hide their dark, secretive, unhealed areas. I can well understand why. There really are few safe places where one can go and find those who understand the importance of confidentiality and who are called to help others in need of healing. The Church should be that place.

All of us need to continually ask God to open our blind eyes, humbly receive God's truth, and trust Him to bring change in our lives. Is that not why He gave His Son to save us from Satan, the father of lies of those who are perishing? It is time to stop believing we can get away with secret shameful ways, when the Word of God says everything will come into the light.

God knows every move we make, every word we speak, and every thought we think. It's so important and more beneficial to bring any secret into the light yourself, rather than wait for God to expose it. It's all about light and darkness. *'Eyes open'* means allowing the light of the truth in. This is God's domain. *'Eyes closed'* blocks out light and invites darkness and deception in. This is Satan's domain. The scary thing is we make our own choices as to how we want to live life, either with eyes open or eyes closed, although sometimes it's a bit of both.

Living in darkness, or the shadows, will not result in us being fruitful either as an individual follower of Jesus, or as a leader in the Church. Whatever our position in life and whatever our background and educational training, I want us to ask ourselves these questions:

1. Are we continuing in the footsteps of the early Christians?
2. Are we seeking the continuous filling of the Holy Spirit?
3. Are we continuing the work of Jesus here on earth?
4. Are we setting captives free as Jesus did?
5. Are we wanting to hear those amazing words, "Well done good and faithful servant?"

God has a plan for the healing of His people and the land, as He prophesied to the people of Israel in Jeremiah 33:6.

> *'Nevertheless, I will bring health and healing to it; (meaning the city and the land) I will heal my people and will let them enjoy abundant peace and security.' (Jeremiah 33:6)*

Didn't Jesus come to establish His Kingdom on earth? Let's remember it is His Kingdom and His Church. We are His servants, and we are called to do His will. I often wonder if we understand what God wants of us in His Kingdom. As God's representatives for truth on earth, are we focused on 'His Kingdom' or 'my church'? As a disciple of Jesus, are we adhering to His teaching and proclaiming the Kingdom of God to the nations? Or have we lost sight of Jesus' teachings, especially in some specific areas of discipleship like healing, correction, and spiritual freedom?

God's plan has always been to restore His Church by fully opening spiritual eyes to His truth. This is an invitation to every committed Christian to look carefully at the healing ministry of Jesus and compare what the Word of God says against what is being taught, or not taught, in some circles about healing and deliverance. Are there truths we are being robbed of?

Isaiah 61 and Luke 4 from verse 14 describe the deliverance ministry of Jesus in 'setting captives free' and releasing people from bondages. Let us not be fearful of these words which actually describe about one third of Jesus' healing ministry. Jesus came, not only for our salvation but also to set us free from the grip of the enemy of our souls. To 'set us free' is to be delivered from a yoke of slavery. Because this is seldom spoken about, the unknown can be scary and many people remain in the clutches of the enemy, never able to do the will of God effectively.

It is for freedom that Christ has set us free. Stand firm, then, and do not let yourselves be burdened again by a yoke of slavery. (Galatians 5:1)

We will be known by our fruit, and there is only one true vine in which this can be achieved. Our fruit is not the multitudes that come and listen to a dynamic preacher. Our fruit should rather be reaching the lost, helping the poor, healing the spiritually poor, and delivering those in bondage to demonic forces. How many in our churches are not 'free'? How many church leaders are not 'free'?

My hope is that this book will result in spiritually closed eyes being opened. My prayer is that this book will help many to find freedom and fullness in Christ and become effective leaders and saints as true disciples of Jesus Christ.

Chapter 1
Light in the Darkness

I love a Kingdom based ministry. I believe that when we bring people together from various denominations to serve God as one Body, it creates a powerful and unique opportunity for God's Kingdom. Even with all our apparent differences, our respect for each other, unity, love, and acceptance seem to draw the presence of the Spirit of God. I love to see a willingness in people from different denominations to eagerly rub shoulders together and learn from each other. There is such a 'richness' of God's presence when we get together in that way.

In my country, South Africa, the apartheid system started falling away after 1994, and the new ANC government was established. Old laws were being abolished and new laws were bringing more freedom of movement and opportunities into our country's nations. My search to go deeper with God was churning away within me at that time. Black people were moving into the inner city where my wife and I were ministering. Change was happening in the physical world, bringing a wonderful new and challenging spiritual dynamic.

It was tough at first, well, maybe I should say awkward rather than tough. The first thing we needed to work on, in our inner-city congregation, was relationship between races. It was an unbelievably beautiful experience that we would never forget. What a privilege it was!

Understandably, trust was a huge issue. Once trust was earned, however, we were able to bond and deepen our relationships. Within two months, God helped us relate as a 'family', but doing personal prayer ministry was different. We had to learn how to minster by understanding the different backgrounds, cultures and viewpoints we had. It was, to say the least, a humbling experience for everyone. We spoke about our experiences, including all the pain and the abuses we had suffered.

As we listened, we gained understanding of each other, black and white, of who 'you' are and who 'I' am. We asked for forgiveness, and we forgave each other. We cried with sorrow and shame, and we laughed at the foolishness of our misunderstanding of each other. We were angry together at our blindness, which had allowed the enemy of our souls to keep us apart in mistrust.

God was deep at work in the lives of people in our congregation. He was opening our eyes to beautiful new friendships as they developed. We grieved about the loss and pain apartheid had caused. In the past we had closed our eyes, making enemies of each other. God, by His amazing grace, was now restoring His Body in the inner city of Pretoria.

I asked the Lord to give me a black friend. He gave me Ayanda Mahola. We developed a friendship in the Lord which we still have today. Ayanda taught me so much about both the good and the ungodly aspects of black rural mind-sets and culture. It is a process which continues to this day. He is a real son in the house.

Something Missing

Those were amazing days of learning. I found that, although God was doing remarkable things in our ministry, we found that there was still something missing. We were struggling to know how to free people from demonic oppression, the result of growing up in this culture where Freemasonry, humanism, materialism, witchdoctors, ancestral worship, sacrifices and other forms of occult were all part of people's normal life. People were saved and delivered to the point of our limited understanding. The people we ministered to were forgiven, born again by the Spirit of God, but still in bondage to demonic spirits.

It was a steep learning curve, not always knowing whether we were doing the right thing. In some cases, we had no success at all. Our cry was, "Lord, how do we set Your people free from demonic strongholds?" Much prayer, asking the Lord these vital questions, followed.

The same questions arose through the telephone ministry we established in 1986, called 'Telefriend'. But this time the question arose of why the Church was not setting captives free. We received thousands of calls and led many thousands to salvation. Many callers were referred to churches around the country for follow up prayer ministry, but many Church leaders would have readily confessed they did not know how to help these people.

Through a lack of equipping, our eyes were spiritually closed to understanding the truth. Our ministry was incomplete, so our search for help intensified. This, I may add, does not just apply to our experience within the South African culture. It's an issue everywhere in the world. God used our situation at the time to highlight and open our eyes to His Word that the Messiah will set us free from various blockages of spiritual oppression. Jesus confirmed this (Luke 4:17-21), as He quoted the well-known passage from Isaiah Chapter 61. People love to quote this scripture, but it needs to be applied.

> *The Spirit of the Sovereign LORD is on me, because the LORD has anointed me to preach good news to the poor. He has sent me to bind up the brokenhearted, to proclaim freedom for the captives and release from darkness for the prisoners, to proclaim the year of the LORD'S favor and the day of vengeance of our God, to comfort all who mourn. (Isaiah 61:1-2)*

By God's grace, Beryl and I met Peter and Fiona Horrobin from Ellel Ministries in the UK while they were visiting South Africa in 1998. Over a hasty twenty-minute cup of tea together, they described their prayer ministry. It was exactly what was on our hearts. They were already doing exactly what we wanted to learn to do. God spoke so deeply into our hearts that we knew our lives were about to change.

By June 2000 we had heard God's call on our lives, resigned from the pastorate and travelled in total faith to Ellel Ministries in the UK to prepare for whatever He had for our future. It was an eighteen-month journey of equipping and healing for us both. This was our first experience of personal healing since the time we had received salvation.

The Lord spoke a sobering word right into my spirit one morning. I was having a prayer time with Him, and He said, *"I want to you to establish Ellel Ministries in Africa, but I cannot use you as you are."* It was a shock, but I knew He was right. I had a lot of sorting out to do in my own life. I immediately said, "Yes Lord, I am willing", and the journey of restoration began. I will take a more in depth look at this in a later chapter.

As a Christian, with eyes wide open to God and to the sensitivity of knowing right and wrong, but still living part of my life outside of the will of God, it demanded much humility, honesty, and repentance to acknowledge the truth. God hates sin, but God loves the repentant son or daughter in His Kingdom. Jesus tells us that, when we approach God in humility and sincerity, our Father in Heaven hears our plea and sees our heart.

> *He who belongs to God hears what God says. The reason you do not hear is that you do not belong to God". (John 8:47)*

With the assurance that all who belong to God hear what He says, we can approach the throne of God, kneel before our Maker and plead for mercy in His Son Jesus' name. I suggest you find a quiet place. Speak your heart to God and commit to walking through the process of healing.

Is there Light in the Darkness?

> *Your eye is the lamp of your body. When your eyes are good, your whole body also is full of light. But when they are bad, your body also is full of darkness. See to it, then, that the light within you is not darkness. Therefore, if your whole body is full of light, and no part of it dark, it will be completely lighted, as when the light of a lamp shines on you. (Luke 11:34-36)*

The metaphor Jesus is using in Luke 11:34-36 about our eyes being good applies to our spiritual lives. These words of

Jesus, *"See to it, then, that the light within you is not darkness"* (Luke 11:35) ring in my ears! Perhaps He means us to do this on a regular basis and ask ourselves the two questions, "How much light do I have?" and "How much darkness am I harboring?" The relative amount of light and darkness will influence our choices and determine the way we live our life.

If I do realize that there is an area of darkness in my life, what should I do about it? Should I confess my dark, shameful secrets and allow light to come into my life? Or should I try to get rid of the darkness some other way, without confessing my secrets? The Scriptures often refers to *'this dark world'* and Jesus publicly announces, *"I am the light of the world"*. The truth is that any unconfessed sin is darkness, and it will always have a hold on me, as long as it remains unconfessed. But if I deal with the dark areas of my life, I will have *'the light of life'* and I *'will never walk in darkness'* again.

> *When Jesus spoke again to the people, he said, "I am the light of the world. Whoever follows me will never walk in darkness, but will have the light of life. (John 8:12)*

Taking Responsibility

One of the things Christians often struggle with is taking responsibility for their own spiritual walk and growth. They want to be fed, like babies, and are quite ready to open their mouths and receive a spoon of whatever tastes or sounds good. The cry of love from Jesus makes it clear that we all have a responsibility, *"See to it... "*. In other words, have discernment about what you are fed spiritually. This is for your own good.

How easy is it to be spiritually discerning? I have found that even mature Christians can be deceived. Reflecting on my life from the time of my salvation at the age of forty, now thirty-eight years later, I well remember the unwise and irresponsible things I did that caused heartache to myself and others. Even though my eyes had been opened to the Lordship of Jesus in my life, there were times when I chose to close my eyes and let darkness in again.

Once darkness is in, it's a tough fight to get it out, so the light of Jesus may shine brightly again. The enemy of our souls loves darkness. He wants to drag us, entice us, lure us and deceive us with lies into his trap of darkness and bondage. All this effort on his part is to distract us from the light of the Lord.

Truth can only flow into our lives when we choose to open our eyes. This is what Jesus meant by saying, *"See to it, then, that the light within you is not darkness"*. The enemy (Satan) hates the true light and will do anything in His power to stop us from receiving the truth of the Gospel of Jesus Christ.

We may find ourselves in a place where we are surrounded by darkness and unsavory characters. Our responsibility is to keep away from ungodly places and things, lest the temptation is too great, and we succumb to allowing darkness in. What our eyes linger on may tempt our body to do what we do not want to do. Do not let your eyes cause you to sin.

Spiritual Eyes Opened

The Book of Acts records how the Apostle Paul explained his conversion experience to King Agrippa, telling him how Jesus had appeared to him on the road to Damascus. At that time his name was Saul, and his spiritual eyes were totally closed to his ungodly actions against God's people, which were consequently against God Himself. He was struck blind and could not see where he was going. But, although his physical eyes had been closed, Jesus opened his spiritual eyes and allowed the truth of God to flow into his heart. Here is his testimony.

> *About noon, O king, as I was on the road, I saw a light from heaven, brighter than the sun, blazing around me and my companions. We all fell to the ground, and I heard a voice saying to me in Aramaic, 'Saul, Saul, why do you persecute me? It is hard for you to kick against the goads.' (Meaning: losing battle) "Then I asked, 'Who are you, Lord?' 'I am Jesus, whom you are persecuting,' the Lord replied. 'Now get up and stand on your feet. I have appeared to you to appoint you as a servant and as a witness of what you have seen of me and what I will show you. I will rescue you from your own people and from the Gentiles. I am sending you to them to open their eyes and turn them from darkness to light, and from the power of Satan to God, so that they may receive forgiveness of sins and a place among those who are sanctified by faith in me.' (Acts 26:13-18)*

Saul got up from the ground, with his physical eyes now closed, but his spiritual eyes opened. We learn in Acts Chapter 9 that Jesus then ordered Ananias to go to Saul and pray for him, so he could have his physical sight restored. It is interesting that Ananias called Saul 'brother'. Saul, once hated by the Jews, was truly now a brother in God's Kingdom.

> But the Lord said to Ananias, "Go! This man is my chosen instrument to carry my name before the Gentiles and their kings and before the people of Israel. I will show him how much he must suffer for my name." Then Ananias went to the house and entered it. Placing his hands on Saul, he said, "Brother Saul, the Lord—Jesus, who appeared to you on the road as you were coming here—has sent me so that you may see again and be filled with the Holy Spirit." (Acts 9:15-17)

Paul's powerful testimony to King Agrippa illustrates how a person can live with physical eyes open, believing they are doing the right thing, but be blinded to God's will and His ways for their life. Hearing this testimony should have been enough to bring the king to an understanding of the saving grace of Jesus, but his spiritual sight was totally closed. Although he had heard about all the amazing accounts of the healings Paul and the disciples were doing, it was as if he had absolutely no concept of a living God. His lifelong idol worship made no space for any other deity. If only he had listened with his heart!

> I pray also that the eyes of your heart may be enlightened in order that you may know the hope to which he has called you, the riches of his glorious inheritance in the saints. (Ephesians 1:18)

Because of pride, the king chose to ignore Paul's testimony of the power of God. Instead, Festus, who was with the King at the time and having the same prideful spirit, shouted out to

Paul: *"You are out of your mind, Paul!"* he shouted. *"Your great learning is driving you insane."* When King Agrippa and Festus joined in ungodly agreement with each other, they chose to close their spiritual eyes to the truth that Paul was describing. This is an example of what can sometimes happen in the Church.

Influence from the teaching of those in authority, even though it has not been tested against God's Word, is able to change how people view the truth of the Gospel. They hear good teaching which draws them towards God, but, if that truth is mixed with some false teaching, yes, they may still be drawn toward God, but, at the same time, their eyes are firmly closed to important aspects within God's truth.

Whether teaching is presented from a legalistic or from a liberal, compromised view, the result will be the same. It will cause the eyes of our understanding to be blurred to the real truth of the Gospel. When we open our hearts to receive Jesus as Lord of our lives, it is wonderful how God opens our spiritual eyes to His truth. So, how tragic it is to have them subtly dimmed and even closed altogether by teaching that is wrong!

Effective Disciples not Religious Practices

"How can these teachers be giving me false teaching? They have studied the Bible for years?" people may protest. I say, they may have studied the Bible thoroughly, having read Genesis to Revelation many times, and may be able to quote to you from every chapter and verse, but I wonder if it has become just a religious practice. Does their study of the Bible relate the Word of God to everyday life and lead to healing the sick or setting captives free?

I am quite sure that the Church of Jesus Christ was never intended to be a place where religious people fear God's wrath if they don't go to church or pay their tithes. It was intended to be a place where disciples are trained and equipped with the power of God to continue the work of Jesus here on earth.

Because everyone in a church setting is at different stages of growth, I realize that not everyone is living life with their spiritual eyes open. But we need to ask some important questions here. Firstly, are the leaders teaching the full truth of God and the full Gospel of Jesus that is in the Bible? And secondly, are the individual Christians in the church studying the Bible and then asking questions if they are not hearing about what's written in it?

In a world that is growing increasingly darker day by day, there are challenges, distractions and temptations for us as Christians, if we want to live life God's way. Now, more than ever, discernment is essential to our survival. Living life with our eyes half open to the truth is no different to living life with our eyes half closed to sin. We must know the full truth.

The Role of Leadership in the Church

I love the Church. It was established by Jesus to continue His work on earth. I see the love in the Church, and the amazing messages they produce week after week. Some congregations feed the needy or have a school or hospital attached to their church. Yet, it seems to me that many churches are not thinking beyond preaching sermons and having home groups. But are these the only activities where Jesus would want us to be concentrating our efforts?

People sometimes look for leaders who are known to be 'lovely' people. They may look for someone who is 'their' type of leader. Well, perhaps the truth is that they themselves are the sort of Christian who likes to compromise by mixing a bit of sin and ungodliness with a bit of righteousness. This is why they like a leader who does the same. But compromise in a Christian's life is the first sign of backsliding and leads to a steady spiritual decline.

If people are impressed by leaders because of their superior education or their theological degrees, but not because they are filled with the Holy Spirit, they will inevitably end up in a church of 'dry bones', where it will be 'all Word and no Spirit'. In this kind of church, the people are more overawed by human cleverness than God's wisdom. They feel that they themselves lack enough knowledge to question anything that is taught by such leaders and may fail to exercise discernment.

Far more important than the formal educational qualification they might have is whether church leaders give life-changing messages, love the Lord with all their heart and are filled with the Holy Spirit. Do they have a passion for souls and setting captives free? Are they vulnerable enough to be open about their own weaknesses, and do they express their total reliance on the Holy Spirit? The disciples of Jesus had no formal education, yet they were powerful in the Word and Holy Spirit anointing (Acts 4:13). That's my idea of the best kind of church leader.

If a leader confesses that he or she has little knowledge of the healing ministry of Jesus, due to not having such teaching at the seminary, college or university they attended, but that they would love to learn more, that's a leader who would certainly get my attention.

All too often, I'm sad to admit, leaders rely on their personality, charisma and even their knowledge of the Word of God to get them through week after week. They often ignore or minimize the scriptures on the 'born again' salvation process, the need for repentance, being baptized, being filled with the Holy Spirit, speaking in tongues, discipling for healing and equipping for works of service to continue the ministry of Jesus.

I believe that if we are not teaching the full Gospel and we are only giving half-truths, we are out of line with Jesus' message of reconciling man to God, and we are robbing God's people of the spiritual freedom Jesus promised and which He died for. We are closing their eyes to truth, instead of opening their eyes to *all* of the truth that there is. If our denomination believes in half-truths, and not the truth from God's perspective, does the fear of losing our pension prevent us from making things right with God and standing for truth? How will we answer when we stand before God one day?

Church leaders are clearly instructed to equip God's people under their care about how to reach their full potential and maturity in Christ. They are called and gifted by God to prepare and equip those people for effective Kingdom living.

It was he (Jesus) who gave some to be apostles, some to be prophets, some to be evangelists, and some to be pastors and teachers to prepare God's people for works of service, so that the body of Christ may be built up until we all reach unity in the faith and in the knowledge of the Son of God and become mature, attaining to the whole measure of the fullness of Christ. Then we will no longer be infants, tossed back and forth by the waves, and blown here and there by every wind of teaching and by the cunning and craftiness of men in their deceitful scheming. Instead, speaking the truth in love, we will in all things grow up into him who is the Head, that is, Christ. From him the whole body, joined and held together by every supporting ligament, grows and builds itself up in love, as each part does its work. (Ephesians 4:11-14)

The Challenge to be a Disciple

If we are called, born again by the Spirit of God, and equipped to do Jesus' will, we are His disciples today, just as much as the disciples we read about in the Gospels. A disciple is one who believes in Jesus, follows Him, obeys His teaching, tells others about the Good News and sets captives free, just as Jesus taught His disciples. Am I really the disciple Jesus wants me to be?

Therefore go and make disciples of all nations, baptizing them in the name of the Father and of the Son and of the Holy Spirit, and teaching them to obey everything I have commanded you. And surely I am with you always, to the very end of the age."
(Matthew 28:19-20)

So they set out and went from village to village, preaching the gospel and healing people everywhere. (Luke 9:6)

He (Jesus) appointed twelve—designating them apostles—that they might be with him and that he might send them out to preach and to have authority to drive out demons. (Mark 3:14)

We may be in a church, but are our eyes open or closed? If our eyes are closed to the full truth of the gospel, we are probably living with darkness in us.

'See to it, then, that the light within you is not darkness'. (Luke 11:35)

I encourage you to ask the Lord to open your spiritual eyes as you read His Word. My prayer is that as you read this book, your eyes will be opened to spiritual truth in new and relevant ways.

A well-known chorus starts with the words, *'I was once in darkness now my eyes can see. I was lost but Jesus sought and found me.'* In the next chapter I will share more of my journey from darkness into the light.

Chapter 2
From Darkness to Light

Before I surrendered my heart to Jesus, I was not going through any major crisis to make me look for a 'higher power'. I did not know that my eyes were spiritually closed, because I had no real understanding of the Kingdom of light or the Kingdom of darkness. I did, however, long to fill a constant gnawing, empty space inside me. I was looking for answers to questions without knowing what those questions were. I certainly knew I was not my own Savior.

I went to church every so often and felt better for it afterwards. I sort of believed in Jesus, His virgin birth, that He was crucified and died on the cross for our sins, that on the third day He rose again, and after appearing to many people and His disciples, was taken into heaven. So, I thought I was a Christian.

Although I had a good belief system, it was just head knowledge. A knowledge of the Christian faith did not make me a Christian. I had an attraction to the Christian faith, and I thought I was a Christian, but I was not. My problem was that I never had a personal relationship with Jesus that connected my spirit to His Spirit. It was my head connecting to my own thoughts, feeling and desires.

The Christianity I believed in was distant and, for some reason, rather threatening. I gravitated towards people with a similar mindset to me, who shared the same unhealthy sentiments about Christians, the Church and God, and sometimes, justifiably so, saw Christians as rather odd. The danger with such agreements, was that it gave me false sense of security that I was not alone in the way I perceived religion. We sort of convinced ourselves we didn't need or want anything to do with God. So, we had a total lack of understanding about God as our source, provider and protector.

We relied totally on our own soulish ability to live life. The added danger here was that the choices we made put us right into the hands of the prince of this world – Satan, the father of lies and his demonic forces. We opened ourselves up to do his will and carry out his schemes. We became critical, irritable, and secretive. We lied about things and even hurt those we loved. I know that, without a plumb line to our life and no fear of consequences, we can constantly be searching for something to fill that void. It could be cigarettes, alcohol, drugs or sexual satisfaction outside of marriage.

I know that I know something happened in my heart when Ivan led me in a prayer to confess my sins and ask Jesus to come and live in me. That was the moment I was translated from my worldly status into God's Kingdom. I was rescued by the King of kings from the enemy's hold on me. That was the moment when I was 'born again'.

Two Kingdoms

To understand what happened to me at that moment, we need to firstly realize that the earth, in which we live, has two spiritual kingdoms operating within it, the Kingdom of God and the Kingdom of Satan. Satan's kingdom is often referred as the 'kingdom of darkness', 'this dark world' or simply 'the world'. When Jesus was teaching His disciples to pray, He included in the prayer that we should ask God that His Kingdom come.

This, then, is how you should pray: "Our Father in heaven, hallowed be your name, your kingdom come, your will be done on earth as it is in heaven. Give us today our daily bread. Forgive us our debts, as we also have forgiven our debtors. And lead us not into temptation, but deliver us from the evil one." For if you forgive men when they sin against you, your heavenly Father will also forgive you. But if you do not forgive men their sins, your Father will not forgive your sins. (Matthew 6:9-15)

You may ask the question, "Where is this Kingdom of God?" Jesus gives us the answer.

Once, having been asked by the Pharisees when the kingdom of God would come, Jesus replied, "The kingdom of God does not come with your careful observation, nor will people say, 'Here it is,' or 'There it is,' because the kingdom of God is within you." (Luke 17:20-21)

God Loves the World

It is good to remind ourselves that we were all born into the world with worldly ways, thoughts, desires and deeds, but that it was God's plan to save us and reconcile us to Himself.

"<u>For God so loved the world</u> that he gave his one and only Son, that whoever believes in him shall not perish but have eternal life. (John 3:16)

The reason Jesus came to earth was to redeem those who are lost, to mend the broken-hearted, to heal the sick, to preach the Kingdom of God and release people from the power of Satan. Before returning to heaven, Jesus released His Church to continue His work here on earth. It is now our calling to love as Jesus loves and accept others as Jesus accepted us. Our own lives are a testimony of God's saving grace and why we needed a Savior. So, we are called to accept sinners, (although not their sin). God loves the world, and so should we, as members of His Church. People are all created in God's image and likeness. They are all valuable and precious to Him and should be to us.

Sometimes it takes a long time for someone to realize they need a Savior. Perhaps you have relatives or friends who have not yet committed their lives to Jesus. If so, pray, asking God our Father for His hand of mercy on their lives.

Only One Gate

Jesus explains that salvation, the way to Father God, only comes through Him. There is no other way.

Jesus answered, "I am the way and the truth and the life. No-one comes to the Father except through me". (John 14:6)

This statement by Jesus sets Christianity apart from all other religions which claim to offer a way of salvation. It isn't Christians that are saying that. It was Jesus, the Son of God, who said it. The world hates what Jesus said about Himself and what we believe. Jesus warned His disciples about that.

'If the world hates you, keep in mind that it hated me first. If you belonged to the world, it would love you as its own. As it is, you do not belong to the world, but I have chosen you out of the world. That is why the world hates you'. (John 15:18-19)

We cannot compromise the truth. The one and only way to
Heaven is through Jesus. Many will tell us that is too
exclusive, and it doesn't fit their theology. But if Jesus said
it, what other theology can there be? All alternatives are false
and merely human ideas. Jesus said the gate, or the door, to
salvation is narrow, in other words, exclusive of any other
way. But because of their pride and stubbornness, people
want to create their own man-made gate.

> *Someone asked him (Jesus), "Lord, are only a few*
> *people going to be saved?" He said to them, "Make*
> *every effort to enter through the narrow door,*
> *because many, I tell you, will try to enter and will*
> *not be able to. Once the owner of the house gets up*
> *and closes the door, you will stand outside knocking*
> *and pleading, 'Sir, open the door for us.' "But he*
> *will answer, 'I don't know you or where you come*
> *from.' "Then you will say, 'We ate and drank with*
> *you, and you taught in our streets.' "But he will*
> *reply, 'I don't know you or where you come from.*
> *Away from me, all you evildoers!' (Luke 13:23-27)*

God did not say that He only loved '*some*' people in the
world. No, He loves every person in the world. He may not
agree with their behavior, but He loves them, because they
are all created in His image and likeness. Jesus said He was
the good shepherd who knew His sheep and whose sheep
knew Him. But He also had other sheep that were not in His
sheepfold. He had to bring them also. They would listen to
His voice and become part of the flock of sheep under one
shepherd (John 10:14-16). If we were not in Jesus' sheepfold,
but we make a heart commitment and receive Him as Lord of

our whole life, an incredible spiritual dynamic takes place. It happens when we ask Jesus to forgive our sins and we say "yes" to Jesus.

We were all in the kingdom of darkness. But the moment we believed and accepted Jesus Christ as our Lord and Savior, we were supernaturally rescued from the kingdom of darkness and lifted supernaturally into the Kingdom of His glorious light. We are brought into the Kingdom of God with Jesus as its King. The King of kings and the Lord of lords.

For he has rescued us from the dominion of darkness and brought us into the kingdom of the Son he loves. (Colossians 1:13)

Jesus confirms that Christians, those who have received Jesus into their hearts, still live in this world, but they are no longer of this world.

I have given them your word and the world has hated them, for they are not of the world any more than I am of the world. My prayer is not that you take them out of the world but that you protect them from the evil one. They are not of the world, even as I am not of it. (John 17:14-16)

Being Born Again

That moment of believing in Jesus or 'being born again' was explained by Jesus to Nicodemus in John Chapter 3. It seems Jesus took 'believing' to another level, because He not only wanted us to believe, but to 'see' the Kingdom of God in operation in our lives.

Now there was a man of the Pharisees named Nicodemus, a member of the Jewish ruling council. He came to Jesus at night and said, "Rabbi, we know you are a teacher who has come from God. For no one could perform the miraculous signs you are doing if God were not with him." In reply Jesus declared, "I tell you the truth, no one can see the kingdom of God unless he is born again." "How can a man be born when he is old?" Nicodemus asked. "Surely he cannot enter a second time into his mother's womb to be born!" Jesus answered, "I tell you the truth, no one can enter the kingdom of God unless he is born of water and the Spirit. Flesh gives birth to flesh, but the Spirit gives birth to spirit. You should not be surprised at my saying, 'You must be born again.'" (John 3:1-7)

He wanted us to be born again by His Spirit, which is the beginning of us being able to do the work He did. When we are born again, God allows us to do the same work as Jesus and we use His name to do it. Being filled with the Holy Spirit, which is an additional experience, is a hugely important aspect to the effectiveness of our Christian walk.

Many would say we receive the Holy Spirit when we are born again. To a degree that would be correct. That is because, by our invitation, we invite Jesus to come and live in us by His Holy Spirit. Jesus is sitting at the right hand of God the Father in the heavenly realm as He continuously intercedes for us. Shortly after Jesus was taken up into Heaven, God gave us another Comforter, the Holy Spirit. The function of the Holy

Spirit is to mingle with our human spirit, making it alive to Christ.

Nicodemus said that he knew Jesus was a teacher who came from God, because of the miraculous signs He was doing. But Jesus responded by seeming to change the subject. He made an important statement that He wanted every believer to understand. To enter the Kingdom of God, we have to be 'born again'. The first birth is our physical birth. I believe that, when Jesus refers to being *'born of water'*, He is referring to our physical birth and does not refer to adult baptism, and definitely not to baby sprinkling or dedication. Verse 6 explains what it means to be 'born again', and that our second birth is a spiritual re-birth of our human spirit.

'Flesh gives birth to flesh, but the Spirit gives birth to spirit. (John 3:6)

Remember, at the fall of man, mankind became separated from God when Adam and Eve obeyed Satan and came under his control. Jesus came to restore, through Himself, our spiritual connection with God. Nicodemus was confused about having two births, so Jesus explains. Verse 6 explains the two births, one physical and the second spiritual.

Jesus explained that Spirit (God's Spirit) gives birth to spirit (human spirit). To be born again by the Spirit of God is God's investment of His Son into our individual lives. It is reserved for all those who believe, are baptized as a believer through our own free will choice and then choose to live life under the Lordship of Jesus Christ.

Peter reminded the believers that they are now born again and that their human spirit was made new and imperishable, prepared for everlasting life.

> *For you have been born again, not of perishable seed, but of imperishable, through the living and enduring word of God. (1 Peter 1:23)*

Guidelines to a Born-Again Process

If you have not yet invited Jesus into your heart to be your Lord and Savior, I urge you, consider taking the following steps which will help deepen your relationship with Jesus. Yes, you may already believe in Jesus and even go to a church every Sunday, but if you have not spoken out the words from your heart inviting Jesus to come live in you, you will have missed this vital step.

As already mentioned, Beryl and I attended a traditional church in Windhoek, Namibia, but in hindsight, we were still in the world - for twenty-eight years! I was serving in the church in Port Elizabeth and Windhoek for years but never hearing about the saving grace of Jesus Christ. My experience makes me so keenly aware that there are many church goers who have never actually given their lives to Jesus and been born again.

Should you desire in your heart to give your life to Jesus, here is a guideline for your prayer request to the Lord.

Take your time to:

> Confess to Jesus you are a sinner, *"for all have sinned and fall short of the glory of God" (Romans 3:23)*

Ask Jesus to forgive you of your sin. *'He told them, "This is what is written: The Christ will suffer and rise from the dead on the third day, and repentance and forgiveness of sins will be preached in his name to all nations, beginning at Jerusalem.'* (Luke 24:46-47)

Forgive us our sins, for we also forgive everyone who sins against us. (Luke 11:4)

There is a condition to receiving forgiveness from God. We have to forgive others – no matter how hard that may sometimes be. *'For if you forgive men when they sin against you, your heavenly Father will also forgive you. But if you do not forgive men their sins, your Father will not forgive your sins.'* (Matthew 6:14-15)

Repent – Turn around when temptation faces you. Make the decision to stop sinning. You may slip up a couple of times, but make a concerted effort to stop all ungodly talk and practice. *'From that time on Jesus began to preach, "Repent, for the kingdom of heaven is near."'* (Matthew 4:17)

Invite Jesus to come live in your heart, Jesus said, *"Here I am! I stand at the door and knock.* (Jesus knocks, He is always hoping you would respond). *If anyone hears my voice and opens the door. I will come in and eat with him, and he with me".* (Revelations 3:20)

Eating with Jesus speaks of a two-way relationship. Holman Hunt painted a famous picture of this verse with a door which only had one door handle and it was on the inside. Only you, using your own free will, can open the door to your heart and invite Jesus in.

Having said that prayer, the Bible says you have been saved by faith – not by feeling. Believe it and enjoy fellowship with Jesus.

Tell at least three people of your decision to accept Jesus as your Lord and Savior. This will strengthen your relationship with Jesus and give you confidence to speak it out. *"Whoever acknowledges me before men, I will also acknowledge him before my Father in heaven. But whoever disowns me before men, I will disown him before my Father in heaven." (Matthew 10:32-33)*

Welcome to God's Kingdom

Once you have come before God, humbled yourself, asked Him to come and live in your heart, He is faithful, and He will do just that. At that moment, He comes into your heart by His Holy Spirit – the Spirit of God. His Spirit touches your human spirit, and you are born again by the Spirit of the Living God – as I have already explained. You have now given your life over to God through Jesus Christ our Lord. Rejoice, give thanks with a grateful heart, for you are now alive to Christ.

You are saved, not by feeling, but by faith. Jesus has rescued you. He has snatched you from the fire (Jude 1:23) and transported you from the kingdom of Satan into the Kingdom of God. For this reason, Jesus came to earth, to reconcile us to God our Father and to separate us from the world and its sinful ways.

Not only is this so, but we also rejoice in God through our Lord Jesus Christ, through whom we have now received reconciliation. (Romans 5:11)

Jesus loves us so much, in spite of all our wrongdoing. This is God's grace. Let's not mess with it!

If, for the first time, you have gone before the Lord and prayed through each step in the above prayer to invite Jesus into your heart, may I welcome you into the Kingdom of God. You no longer belong to the kingdom of this world where Satan rules; you have been spiritually translated into the Kingdom of God where Jesus is King. You and all those reading these words, who have received Jesus as Lord of their lives, are now the prized possessions of Jesus. The good news for you now is that,

> "... you also were included in Christ when you heard the word of truth, the gospel of your salvation. Having believed, you were marked in him with a seal, the promised Holy Spirit, who is a deposit guaranteeing our inheritance until the redemption of those who are God's possession—to the praise of his glory. (Ephesians 1:13-14)

You Now Belong to Christ

Take heart new brothers and sisters in Christ. What has just happened as you earnestly prayed a prayer asking Jesus to come and live in your heart is this, spiritually; you were immediately translated from the kingdom of darkness into the Kingdom of God's glorious light. You are now safely in God's and Jesus' hands, and no one can snatch you from their hands. This is amazing and so comforting.

> Jesus answered, "I did tell you, but you do not believe. The miracles I do in my Father's name speak for me, but you do not believe because you are

not my sheep. My sheep listen to my voice; I know them, and they follow me. I give them eternal life, and they shall never perish; no one can snatch them out of my hand. My Father, who has given them to me, is greater than all; no one can snatch them out of my Father's hand. I and the Father are one." *(John 10:25-30)*

When we invite Jesus into our heart, we receive the presence of God into our human spirit through the indwelling presence of the Holy Spirit.

Jesus replied, "If anyone loves me, he will obey my teaching. My Father will love him, and we will come to him and make our home with him. He who does not love me will not obey my teaching. These words you hear are not my own; they belong to the Father who sent me. "All this I have spoken while still with you. But the Counselor, the Holy Spirit, whom the Father will send in my name, will teach you all things and will remind you of everything I have said to you. (John 14:23-26)

The Spirit himself testifies with our spirit that we are God's children. (Romans 8:16)

And in him you too are being built together to become a dwelling in which God lives by his Spirit. (Ephesians 2:22)

I pray that out of his glorious riches he may strengthen you with power through his Spirit in your inner being, (Ephesians 3:16)

We know that we live in him and he in us, because he has given us of his Spirit. (1 John 4:13)

Receive the Baptism in the Holy Spirit

As new believers our human spirit comes alive again to God through the indwelling presence of His Holy Spirit. There is a deeper experience of God's presence in our life that the Bible refers to as the 'Baptism in the Holy Spirit'. This Baptism or filling with the Holy Spirit comes about as we completely surrender every part of our lives to God and ask Him to fill us and empower us with His Spirit. This empowering is necessary to enable us, His Church, to continue the work of Jesus here on earth.

I baptize you with water for repentance, but he who is coming after me is mightier than I, whose sandals I am not worthy to carry. He will baptize you with the Holy Spirit and fire. (Matthew 3:11)

On the last day of the feast, the great day, Jesus stood up and cried out, "If anyone thirsts, let him come to me and drink. Whoever believes in me, as the Scripture has said, 'Out of his heart will flow rivers of living water'. Now this he said about the Spirit, whom those who believed in him were to receive, for as yet the Spirit had not been given, because Jesus was not yet glorified. (John 7:37-38)

I am going to send you what my Father has promised; but stay in the city until you have been clothed with power from on high. (Luke 24:49)

But you will receive power when the Holy Spirit comes on you; and you will be my witnesses in

*Jerusalem, and in all Judea and Samaria, and to the
ends of the earth. (Acts 1:8)*

*Peter replied, "Repent and be baptized, every one
of you, in the name of Jesus Christ for the
forgiveness of your sins. And you will receive the gift
of the Holy Spirit. The promise is for you and your
children and for all who are far off—for all whom
the Lord our God will call." (Acts 2:38-39)*

Sometimes people receive this Baptism in the Holy Spirit at
the moment of their salvation when they are 'born again'.
Others may receive it later such as in the case of the first
believers in Samaria. They had received Jesus, they were
'baptized' into the name of the Lord Jesus, meaning they
were born again, but they had not yet received the infilling of
the Holy Spirit. They were open to receive all that God had
for them, so when Peter and John placed their hands on them
and prayed for them, they received the Holy Spirit.

*When the apostles in Jerusalem heard that Samaria
had accepted the word of God, they sent Peter and
John to them. When they arrived, they prayed for
them that they might receive the Holy Spirit,
because the Holy Spirit had not yet come upon any
of them; they had simply been baptized into the
name of the Lord Jesus. Then Peter and John placed
their hands on them, and they received the Holy
Spirit. (Acts 8:14-17)*

Jesus wants us to 'see' the Kingdom of God at work in our
lives. It requires that our human spirits be born again and
made new and alive to God. This is the instruction Jesus gave
Nicodemus, who was a 'religious' man, but never saw the

working of God in His life as he saw in Jesus. Jesus, before he began His earthly ministry, submitted himself to John the Baptist for adult baptism and the infilling of the Holy Spirit.

Why should we believe in doing things differently and ignore His instruction because of some incorrect beliefs in the denomination of our own church? Wrong belief systems rob us from the blessings God wants us to have. I encourage you, when reading the Bible, to ask God to open your spiritual eyes to His truth. Ask God to reveal His truth about being born again, about believer's baptism and the infilling of the Holy Spirit.

Opening of Spiritual Eyes Brings Change

When we receive Jesus, our eyes seem to open partially to the Father, but when we receive the Holy Spirit, He opens our spiritual eyes fully and gives us discernment to 'all truth'. For example, when we read the Bible, it will no longer be just words. The Word of God becomes alive to us, and all of a sudden, we sense God speaking to us, through His Word or directly into our spirit while we are in prayer.

> *But when he, the Spirit of truth, comes, he will guide you into all truth. He will not speak on his own; he will speak only what he hears, and he will tell you what is yet to come. (John 16:13)*

How can I forget the day shortly after I gave my heart to Jesus? I was at home, in-between a job change, Beryl was at work and Michael and Janine were at school. I spent the morning in bed 'devouring' Romans. When I got to Romans Chapter 8, the Holy Spirit was opening my new spiritual eyes to the truth, and I got so excited. Have you ever seen a forty-year-old literally jump on his bed with excitement? I was so pleased that I was alone at home, for it must have been quite a sight. But it was the only way, I suppose, that I could release the excitement that had built up in me.

The Bible was no longer just meaningless words, because it had become alive, and God was speaking directly into my spirit. There is no better excitement than that. My outlook on life was changing so much, and my mind was being renewed. I just wanted to follow and obey all that Jesus had for me. I wanted to know what my response should be to the great commission of Jesus.

> *"...go and make disciples of all nations, baptizing them in the name of the Father and of the Son and of the Holy Spirit, and teaching them to obey everything I have commanded you." (Matthew 28:19-20)*

In this chapter I have been talking about what it means to be 'born again' and move out of the Kingdom of Darkness into the Kingdom of Light. In the next chapter we will explore a little more about the origins of the Kingdom of Darkness and why it has so much influence in our lives.

Chapter 3
The Enemy Exposed

Before becoming a Christian, and even during the first few years after inviting Jesus into my life, I had little knowledge about Satan or the spiritual battle engulfing us. I heard few sermons about the nature of this spiritual battle or the active role Christians are called to play in this battle. My eyes have been opened, however, and I now see more clearly how the kingdom of darkness seeks to pervade and affect every part of our lives.

In writing this book, I want to encourage you not to walk in fear of the enemy but to understand his strategy and tactics, so that you can appropriate the victory that Jesus has won for us over this enemy.

We need to recognize the role of Satan and his forces seeking any opportunity to cause misery and hardship to us. His reason? Because every human being is created in God's image and likeness, and for this reason alone, he hates us. The good news is that, when we live life in obedience to God, he has no rights over us. However, let me stress, that does not mean we will not face hardships in life. Hardships often come to strengthen us and help us to grow spiritually.

It is so interesting, when reading the Scriptures, to see references made to light and darkness and the opening and closing of spiritual eyes. To understand this, we need to briefly go back to the time before human beings came on to the scene. Understanding what happened in the beginning will help us to understand what's happening in the world today.

Rebellion in Heaven

Our problems on Earth started right there, in Heaven, even before the creation of mankind. Before being banished from Heaven, Satan seems to have had a brilliant relationship with God. As an archangel, he had authority to perform whatever duties God gave him. In Isaiah 14:12-17, the spiritual forces behind the earthly Kingdom of Babylon are addressed as an archangel, who is referred to as the 'bearer of light' or 'morning star.' In the King James version of the Bible, the translators used the word 'Lucifer', which was a name for the planet Venus.

In a similar passage in Ezekiel 28:12-17, addressed to the spiritual powers behind the ungodly earthly Kingdom of Tyre, this archangel is referred to as an anointed 'guardian cherub'. It would seem that he was the most beautiful of all the angels. Being aware of his beauty opened a door of pride in him. As the Word tell us, *'Pride goes before destruction, a haughty spirit before a fall'* (Proverbs 16:18).

This was certainly the case here. He wooed a third of Heaven's angels into submitting to his influential position, deception and beauty (Revelation 12:4). It seems he was challenging God for sovereignty over the heavenlies and craved worship for himself. He soon learnt the mighty power of God.

Pride demands all the glory. Already one third of all the angels in Heaven were following and worshipping this God-created beauty. Pride has an appetite for attention, and he wanted all of God's angels to follow him. Thus began the start of a rebellion against God. Pride and rebellion are sin. Sin is not tolerated in Heaven. I think God waited just long enough for all the rebellious angels to show their allegiance to Satan publicly before He took action. A third of Heaven's angels who worshipped and followed Lucifer were deceived by his beauty and were subsequently banished from Heaven to Earth.

Fighting for Survival

Jesus was right there at the time of Satan's expulsion from Heaven. Jesus makes mention of His presence in Luke Chapter 10:18. He explained to His disciples that He was there and witnessed the fall of Lucifer. *"I saw Satan fall* like *lightning from heaven"*.

Obviously, Satan lost his position as an archangel and his relationship with God was severed. Now he was God's adversary, an enemy of God, also known as the devil. He not only lost his place in Heaven, but he also lost his authority to exercise his heavenly duties. Earth became his new dwelling place.

Created human beings were now about to enter the scene on earth.

> *Then God said, "Let us make man in our image, in our likeness, and let them rule over the fish of the sea and the birds of the air, over the livestock, over all the earth, and over all the creatures that move along the ground." So God created man in his own image, in the image of God he created him; male and female he created them. When God created man, he made him in the likeness of God. (Genesis 1:26-27)*

*... the LORD God formed the man from the dust of
the ground and breathed into his nostrils the breath
of life, and the man became a living being. Now the
LORD God had planted a garden in the east, in
Eden; and there he put the man he had formed.
(Genesis 2:7-8)*

*But for Adam no suitable helper was found. So the
LORD God caused the man to fall into a deep sleep;
and while he was sleeping, he took one of the man's
ribs and closed up the place with flesh. Then the
LORD God made a woman from the rib he had taken
out of the man, and he brought her to the man. The
man said, "This is now bone of my bones and flesh
of my flesh; she shall be called 'woman,' for she was
taken out of man." (Genesis 2:21-23)*

*He created them male and female and blessed them.
And when they were created, he called them "man."
(Genesis 5:2)*

The devil was there when God came down to earth, took
some dust and formed man. He was also present when God
gave Adam dominion over the earth and a single
commandment to obey.

*The LORD God took the man and put him in the
Garden of Eden to work it and take care of it. And
the LORD God commanded the man, "You are free
to eat from any tree in the garden; but you must not
eat from the tree of the knowledge of good and evil,
for when you eat of it you will surely die." (Genesis
2:15-17)*

When Satan heard that simple instruction which God had given Adam not to eat from the tree in the middle of the garden, I bet his first thought was, *"There must be a loophole somewhere"*. He knew that, in the garden, Adam and Eve's eyes were fully open to God, because they were in a beautiful relationship with God and always obedient to Him.

Now on Earth, the place where you and I live, Satan's lust for power has never ended. He not only wants to control the world, but he wants to destroy anything on earth relating to God, and in particular God's Church. His hate not only includes every believer but every person, because we are all created in the image of God. Even today he wants to abolish and dishonor age old biblical and governmental laws pertaining to purity, marriage, human sexuality, and moral laws, even to the degrading of innocent children.

Authority Given

God had given to Adam and Eve (mankind), authority to rule and reign over all the earth. They would prosper, multiply and live at peace with Him and each other.

> *God blessed them and said to them, "Be fruitful and increase in number; fill the earth and subdue it. Rule over the fish of the sea and the birds of the air and over every living creature that moves on the ground." (Genesis 1:28)*

Lucifer had lost his place of authority in Heaven, and now he saw a place of authority on earth given to mankind. This was a bitter pill for Satan to swallow. He immediately went about devising a plan to steal their authority over all the earth for himself. God's blessings for mankind come largely through obedience, faithfulness, and trust in Him. In giving the directive to Adam not to eat of the fruit in the middle of the garden, God was requiring a willingness to obey Him. This heart attitude attracts God's blessing, whereas disobedience to God attracts the enemy's curse.

Disobedience to God is, in effect, obedience to Satan. When we are disobedient to God, Satan obtains rights over us. When we are obedient to God, we come under God's divine protection (Psalm 91). It's as simple as that. An excellent example of free will choice and its consequences is found in this promise in Deuteronomy.

This day I call heaven and earth as witnesses against you that I have set before you life and death, blessings and curses. Now choose life, so that you and your children may live and that you may love the LORD your God, listen to his voice, and hold fast to him. For the LORD is your life, and he will give you many years in the land he swore to give to your fathers, Abraham, Isaac and Jacob. (Deuteronomy 30:19-20)

Andy's Story

The story of Andy Robinson recorded in his book 'The Choice' (published by Sovereign World) exemplifies how this principle of making right choices still applies today.

As a teenager, Andy Robinson was angry all the time. He found the God stuff at home was choking him. He couldn't play football on Sundays, and he couldn't go to parties. He figured that if his parents loved God so much, that was their choice, but he was making his own choice. They wanted him to commit to God, so in keeping with what he wanted, he decided to commit his life to the devil, to Satan. "Look, to be honest, Satan," he said out loud, "if you can give me all the money and sex and power that I want, frankly you're welcome to any of the soul, spiritual stuff." He didn't realize it at first, but after committing his life to Satan, things definitely got worse. One day he nearly killed one of his brothers with a kitchen knife because he wound him up.

His world finally came crashing down. He found himself homeless, desperate and living in fear on the streets, stealing to support himself. He was out of control and in a downward spiral of destruction. He had made a series of disastrous decisions. He was so addicted to cigarettes and beer that he had started stealing even from those who were trying to show him love and kindness.

After robbing his own father, he knew he could never go back home, never thinking that the consequences of his actions would be that his mother would become ill. He felt nothing and was dead inside. He was out of control and no longer cared about anybody.

He began self-harming. Life was dark and empty. At the age of seventeen, prison became the only safe place from the danger of being abused at night and a refuge from the cold and the hunger.

Later, after experiencing the trauma of a broken marriage and the pain of losing touch with his baby son, his depression steadily increased to the point where he tried to take his own life twice by overdosing, and then a gang also tried to kill him by spiking his drink in a pub.

When a friend at work invited him to church, he never thought he would go, but the fear of being attacked, and the loneliness of having nowhere else to go on a Sunday night, drove him to give it a try. It was a life-changing encounter. He was overwhelmed by the genuine warm welcome, the friendliness, and the love of the young Christians there and their happiness. He understood for the first time that it was about his choice to be in relationship to God. He gave his life to the Lord and the burden of fear and worry drained away. He had feelings again. He was able to sleep.

After a while he experienced a severe spiritual attack from the devil, who was mocking him and claiming his right to Andy's life. He really had taken over Andy's life and led him in paths of destruction.

Fortunately, the elder of the church knew some ladies from Ellel Ministries who were able to help Andy. The spiritual battle was long and difficult because, although he was saved, the enemy still had ground. He had to face the realities of the past and repent of his actions which had caused such deep bondage.

Eventually the battle was won, and he was back in control of his own life. There was no open door anymore. He found prayer worked. He began the process of breaking the coils he had wound around himself through years of abuse, addictions, pain, self-mutilation and the occult.

Following three years at Bible College, with his whole family, Andy became the pastor of a local church in the UK and started reaching out to others with the good news that Jesus can set captives free if they are willing to make right choices.

The Schemer

Simple! Satan has a right to use our disobedient free will choice for his purposes. If we obey him, we will walk right into his web of bondage and become a slave to sin. *'Jesus replied, "Very truly I tell you, everyone who sins is a slave to sin"'* (John 8:34). Satan's plan includes using deception, planting seeds of doubt about God's Word, and enticing us with worldly pleasures such as riches and lusts of the flesh to draw us away from God's blessing.

Adam and Eve, created in God's image and likeness, had an amazing relationship with God. Satan's plan was to break trust in that relationship. If he could lure them into obeying him, it would lead to shame, self-rejection, depression and a host of other self-battering tools. To change their faithful lifestyle of obedience to a place of disobedience would give Satan the right to snatch authority to rule and reign in their lives and in the lives of their descendants.

It's all about our choices. When we sin, we do something that's hostile to God. We step into Satan's territory and give him rights over us. We choose, with our physical eyes wide open, to be disobedient. We then choose to close our spiritual eyes to God, thereby turning our back on the love of God our Creator.

I know some people who don't like using the word 'sin' anymore, but sin is sin, and there is no other name for it. We need to understand and recognize our acts of sin. God views our acts of sin as disobedience, a free will choice against Him. Because we have a free will, God will not stop us, but we are giving Satan permission over our lives. If we don't sin, Satan has no control over us.

The sinful mind is hostile to God. It does not submit to God's law, nor can it do so. Those controlled by the sinful nature cannot please God. You, however, are controlled not by the sinful nature but by the Spirit, if the Spirit of God lives in you. And if anyone does not have the Spirit of Christ, he does not belong to Christ. (Romans 8:7-9)

The Deceiver at Work

When Satan put his plan to the test, he went to Eve and spoke about the beautiful, healthy and rich-looking fruit, dangling it before Eve. I wonder why Adam didn't counsel his wife that she was not to eat this fruit and why he didn't remind her of God's commandment. Why didn't he protect his wife and tell the devil to 'back off'? Because he didn't protect her, it makes him an accessory to her sin. The following Scripture reference tells the story, and it's very important to understand. The event that took place here still has a hold on the world even today.

The woman said to the serpent, "We may eat fruit from the trees in the garden, but God did say, 'You must not eat fruit from the tree that is in the middle of the garden, and you must not touch it, or you will die.'" "You will not surely die," the serpent said to the woman. "For God knows that when you eat of it your eyes will be opened, and you will be like God, knowing good and evil." (Genesis 3:2-5)

The deceiver was at the top of his game. First of all, he persuaded Eve to question what God had said about dying, by saying, "You will not surely die". She may have thought that what the devil said made sense, because dying did not fit in with her idea of God's love and integrity. She probably reasoned that, if she did do something wrong, surely God wouldn't kill her.

Then the devil spoke saying, *"For God knows that when you eat of it your eyes will be opened, and you will be like God, knowing good and evil."* The truth was that Eve's spiritual eyes were already open; they were never closed. But Satan deceived her that there was an additional opening of her eyes which she knew nothing about. He lied to Eve. His intention was to close her eyes to the truth she already had. With eyes wide open, she exercised her free will to believe the devil and disobey God, with the result that her eyes now closed to God's truth.

> *When the woman saw that the fruit of the tree was good for food and pleasing to the eye, and also desirable for gaining wisdom, she took some and ate it. She also gave some to her husband, who was with her, and he ate it. (Genesis 3:6)*

Eve thought she would become wise, but she already was. Oh, what a sly trap that was! The crux of Satan's cunning scheme was unfolding as he had hoped. When Eve ate, nothing happened. With relief she didn't drop down dead as God had said. Was God telling the truth? God had not planned death as part of mankind's existence on earth, but Adam and Eve's disobedience changed everything. Not only would their bodies now have a limited lifespan, but they also had a spiritual separation from God the Father. Their human spirits were now 'dead' to God.

The eyes of Adam and Eve were indeed opened, not to truth but to sin, which they never knew before. Their eyes opened to the realization that disobedience to God exposed their sinful shame, and sin opened the door to the demonic. Not only did they rebel against God, whom they loved, spirits of fear and shame entered their lives, so they hid in the darkness of the trees and covered their shame with fig leaves, hoping God would not find them. Their reaction shows that their eyes were closed to the full truth of God's love, plan and purpose for their lives and for future humanity.

Then the eyes of both of them were opened, and they realized they were naked; so they sewed fig leaves together and made coverings for themselves. Then the man and his wife heard the sound of the LORD God as he was walking in the garden in the cool of the day, and they hid from the LORD God among the trees of the garden. (Genesis 3:7-8)

When our eyes are open to sin and closed to God, we have to wait for the day that our eyes will be opened to God and closed to sin. We have the same choices to make as Adam and Eve. Let us not blame Adam and Eve for their bad choices, because we have the same choices to make.

The choice Adam and Eve made in the garden, with God watching, changed the course of the life God intended for mankind. "Why did God not stop them?" you may ask. The answer to that question is that God is not a controller. Satan is. We have a free will to be obedient to God or be obedient to Satan. Disobedience to God is sin, and when we sin, obviously God is saddened by our choice. But His love for us remains unchanged. He is hoping we will come to our senses, turn from our sin and repent from our ways, so He can forgive us.

"You have said, 'It is futile to serve God. What did we gain by carrying out his requirements and going about like mourners before the LORD Almighty? But now we call the arrogant blessed. Certainly the evildoers prosper, and even those who challenge God escape.'" Then those who feared the LORD talked with each other, and the LORD listened and heard. A scroll of remembrance was written in his presence concerning those who feared the LORD and honored his name. "They will be mine," says the LORD Almighty, "in the day when I make up my treasured possession. I will spare them, just as in compassion a man spares his son who serves him. And you will again see the distinction between the righteous and the wicked, between those who serve God and those who do not. (Malachi 3:14-18)

"No servant can serve two masters. Either he will hate the one and love the other, or he will be devoted to the one and despise the other. You cannot serve both God and Money." (Luke 16:13)

Jesus replied, "If anyone loves me, he will obey my teaching. My Father will love him, and we will come to him and make our home with him. He who does not love me will not obey my teaching. These words you hear are not my own; they belong to the Father who sent me." (John 14:23-24)

Authority Lost

As a result of Satan tempting Eve, and Eve convincing Adam to satisfy the weakness of the flesh and eat of the fruit, there were huge consequences. Adam and Eve switched allegiance to Satan and, by default, handed over to Satan the authority to rule and reign over all the earth. We have all been living with the consequences of that act of disobedience ever since. This is the situation for each and every one of our lives.

We need to understand what happened in Heaven and in the garden to get a grip of what's happening in our lives and who is ruling on earth. Yes, God is in control, but His time to intervene has not yet come. Even Jesus, when speaking to His disciples before His arrest, calls Satan *'the prince of this world'*.

I will not speak with you much longer, for the prince of this world is coming. He has no hold on me. (John 14:30)

With a place of authority to operate as 'Prince of this world', Satan was now in a position to do everything in his power to contend for and oppose everything that is of God. He uses the places of authority given him by individuals, groups and nations to destroy everything that is good and wholesome. His plans and purposes were succinctly summarized by Jesus in John 10:10a:

The thief comes only to steal and kill and destroy. (John 10:10a)

Friendship with the World

Reading God's word, we soon realize how He hates sin. He made us in His image and likeness, and sin has no place in His image and likeness. His great love for us is for us to have the best of life. When we allow anything foreign to His nature into our lives, we block Him from blessing us with the good purposes He has prepared for us on earth. 'The World', which is under the dominion of Satan's kingdom, is forever calling us to a life foreign to God's image and likeness. The enemy plants ideas and desires to tempt us away from the Father until, eventually, we give in to the lusts of the flesh.

> *You adulterers! Don't you realize that friendship with the world makes you an enemy of God? I say it again: If you want to be a friend of the world, you make yourself an enemy of God. (James 4:4 NLT)*

Anything done outside of God's purpose for our lives and bodies gives rights for Satan's demonic forces to have a hold on us. The more we sin, the more we allow the enemy to wrap us up in his web of bondage. Once we are addicted to a sin, the struggle to be free could be a long one. But God has other plans for us. Just as we freely started to sin, freely we must create the desire to fight our way back to God.

If we are ignorant of Satan's ways, we may find out the hard way the consequences of being in 'friendship with the world'. Just as cashiers and those regularly handling genuine notes have a much greater ability to identify fraudulent bank notes, the more we understand God's ways, the easier it will be for us to discern and recognize the enemy's ways.

Like any good commercial salesperson, knowing the strengths and weakness of your own product, as well as the opposition's product, will give you an advantage from a sales point of view. The enemy of our souls fears the one who knows God and know the weakness of the enemy. The words, *'Don't you realize'*, in the above-mentioned verse is asking us a question about our friendship with the world. The question we should ask ourselves should be, "How much of the world do I still have in me?" After giving it careful thought, we may be shocked. Romans 1:18-32 makes for some frightening reading.

To counter and recognize the work of the enemy we need the indwelling presence of the Spirit of God. In Scripture the word 'Spirit', spelt with a capital 'S', would always refer to the Spirit of God or the Holy Spirit (they are the same Spirit). Whereas 'spirit', with a lower case 's', would always refer to either human spirit or evil spirit.

> *For who among men knows the thoughts of a man except the man's spirit within him? In the same way no one knows the thoughts of God except the Spirit of God. We have not received the spirit of the world but the Spirit who is from God, that we may understand what God has freely given us. This is what we speak, not in words taught us by human wisdom but in words taught by the Spirit, expressing spiritual truths in spiritual words. The man without the Spirit does not accept the things that come from the Spirit of God, for they are foolishness to him, and he cannot understand them, because they are spiritually discerned. The spiritual man makes judgments about all things, but he himself is not subject to any man's judgment: "For who has known the mind of the Lord that he may instruct him?" But we have the mind of Christ.*
> *(1 Corinthians 2:11-16)*

This passage makes it quite clear in verse 14 that a person without the 'Spirit' of God would find it quite easy to interpret parts of Scripture from a soulish perspective and be deceived into thinking it to be God's truth. Ministers of the

Gospel not knowing the devil's ways and his scheming principles will probably never set captives free. Even worse, they may lead people into deception and further bondage.

Every born-again Christian is in 'the ministry' and 'a minister' of the Gospel, and should, therefore, be equipped to help others wanting to be free from bondage to the enemy. About one third of Jesus' healing ministry involved delivering people from the claws of Satan. If we don't believe that God's people need to be set free after living in Satan's kingdom of darkness, we are ourselves already in deception, and we need ministry to come out of darkness.

Scripture speaks a lot about how to avoid being caught in the enemy's web. We can learn a lot about the character of Satan and his demonic forces, which are warring continuously against our souls. We don't have to learn lessons of life the hard way. We can study how to live life God's way and realize there are possible consequences if we choose not to obey. The pull towards the world, making it look so attractive to our flesh, is real and tempting. We need to identify these temptations in our lives.

There is no doubt that the struggle for the hearts of mankind is taking place in the heavenlies. Both God and Satan desire to use men and women to do their will. When we belong to Him, God uses us in His Kingdom, despite our frailties. He gives us suitable spiritual armor to wage war against the devil's schemes. The wonderful truth is that God is on our side.

Finally, be strong in the Lord and in his mighty power. Put on the full armor of God so that you can take your stand against the devil's schemes. For our struggle is not against flesh and blood, but against the rulers, against the authorities, against the powers of this dark world and against the spiritual forces of evil in the heavenly realms. (Ephesians 6:10-12)

Satan uses the weakness of people who surrender to his bidding. He makes false promises to fulfil their personal dreams, but there is a cost to others, leading to heartache and destruction. God, on the other hand, uses any kindness that exists in people's hearts, when their desire is to do good to others, without seeking personal reward. He then surprises them by blessing them with their heart's desire. Beryl and I can give testimony to this kind of blessing coming from God again and again.

God's original, amazing plan for mankind was shattered by an act of disobedience to Him, the One who created and molded us with loving hands from the very ground of the earth on which we walk today. God loves His creation, and we are part of it.

God is well aware of Satan's activities and atrocities. Jesus explains his evil and horrifying tactics, as well as God's loving plan and purpose for us who believe in Him (John 10:10-11). The option here is the choice of following a 'thief' who wants no good for us, or of following a 'good shepherd' who cares for us and is even prepared to die that we may have eternal life. In my book it's a no-brainer.

The thief comes only to steal and kill and destroy. I have come that they may have life, and have it to the full. "I am the good shepherd. The good shepherd lays down his life for the sheep. (John 10:10-11)

Satan's plan, in short, is to get you and me away from God the Father through disobedience, which would render us ineffective and no threat to his schemes. I say this, because a well-discipled Christian, healed from past hurts and freed of enemy footholds, can more easily discern the lies of the devil.

If Christians have been equipped and trained to discern the devil's lies, they can pray powerfully, heal the sick, set captives free, and preach truth. Satan fears them. Casual church goers, those living with one foot in the 'world', and those controlled by an addictive lifestyle who are already in bondage, pose no serious threat to Satan at all.

> *(Jesus speaking) From the days of John the Baptist until now, the kingdom of heaven has been forcefully advancing, and forceful men lay hold of it. (Matthew 11:12)*

Obedience can be considered as an act of worship. So, we are either worshipping God or Satan. In these end times, the courts of law are tending toward so-called 'human rights' as a way of judging right from wrong. Judgements that are based on God's moral law and biblical principles are fast disappearing.

The choice on how we live life on earth is ours. Each one of us, on a daily basis, has to test our heart and decide how to live our life. Joshua made up his mind quite emphatically when he needed to make a decision to follow God or the idols of his ancestors and the people in the land around them. We need to do the same.

> *"But if serving the LORD seems undesirable to you, then choose for yourselves this day whom you will*

serve, whether the gods your forefathers served beyond the River, or the gods of the Amorites, in whose land you are living. But as for me and my household, we will serve the LORD." (Joshua 24:15)

This is the choice everyone in the world will have to make at least once during their lifetime. The question is usually asked, "What will happen to those who have never heard the Gospel?" I would say that we all have the ability to have a compassionate or a hard-hearted attitude toward others. We display the good and evil in this way.

I believe God will finally judge what we have done in our lives, whether we have done good or evil to others. We may have to wait to ask God Himself one day how He has decided to deal with all these matters. In the meantime, let God deal with them and look at yourself to see if you are in the faith. One day, when we meet with our Maker, it will be too late for excuses. The enemy's plan is to drag as many as he can away from God into his den of fire.

God's Rescue Plan

In spite of Satan's plan to kill, steal and destroy us, the Church, the economy and every ability God has blessed us with, God has not left us without hope. From the beginning, God had a plan for our rescue from Satan's domination over the world.

For he chose us in him before the creation of the world to be holy and blameless in his sight. (Ephesians 1:4)

God was not surprised when Adam and Eve ate the forbidden fruit. He knew it would happen long before that event in the garden took place. Because God would never force us into His plan, He had to give us free will. We need to make the right choice while living on this planet. Paul explains it this way:

This righteousness from God comes through faith in Jesus Christ to all who believe. There is no difference, for all have sinned and fall short of the glory of God. (Romans 3:22-23)

God's rescue plan came through His Son Jesus, who willingly agreed to descend to earth, live life as a human being without sin and pay the price of our sins by dying on the cross. All who repent of their sins, believe in Jesus and receive Him as Lord and Savior, are brought into the Kingdom of God. Jesus makes this statement in the parable of the lost sheep.

I tell you that in the same way there will be more rejoicing in heaven over one sinner who repents than over ninety-nine righteous persons who do not need to repent. (Luke 15:7)

We were all that lost sheep at one time. Those who first believed were the founding members of His Church in His Kingdom. God's rescue plan was first to reveal His Son Jesus to the twelve and then the seventy-two. God's plan has never stopped until this day. If we choose to receive Jesus as our Lord and Savior, we will be spiritually transported by God out of Satan's kingdom of spiritual darkness and bondage. God will open our eyes to His Kingdom of light, new life and the promise of freedom.

The account of Nicodemus, which we looked at earlier, comes into focus when we speak about God's Kingdom. This is so important. We all have a physical birth date, but do we all have a spiritual birth date? This is an important date. It tells us the day and the year we voluntary received Jesus into our heart and our human spirit was made new, or born again, in Christ Jesus. We are transported out of darkness on that day and we enter the Kingdom of God. It does not matter how many times a day we go to church, because Jesus teaches us that *"no one can see the kingdom of God unless he is born again."*

> *In reply Jesus declared, "I tell you the truth, no one can see the kingdom of God unless he is born again."' (John 3:3)*

In other words, when Adam and Eve disobeyed God, they became dead to God, their spiritual eyes were closed and they were separated from God. Jesus came into the world so that we may be made alive again and reconciled to God.

> *But when the time had fully come, God sent his Son, born of a woman, born under law, to redeem those under law, that we might receive the full rights of sons. Because you are sons, God sent the Spirit of his Son into our hearts, the Spirit who calls out, "Abba, Father." So you are no longer a slave, but a son; and since you are a son, God has made you also an heir. (Galatians 4:4-7)*

This is God's rescue plan and the beginning of our healing process. Now, with Jesus in our hearts, our spiritual eyes can be fully opened to God's truth. I encourage you not to allow anyone with fancy teaching or doctrine to start closing close them again.

In this chapter we have been looking at some truths about the kingdom of the enemy that is arrayed against all Christians. In the next chapter we will look at God's plans for the Church, which is intended to be the expression of God's Kingdom here on the earth.

Chapter 4
God's Plan for His Church

Jesus came to redeem us from out of the Kingdom of darkness into His Kingdom of Light. His plan to do this includes us, His Church. Before ascending into Heaven Jesus commissioned his disciples to continue His work on earth.

The Great Commission

> Then the eleven disciples went to Galilee, to the mountain where Jesus had told them to go. When they saw him, they worshiped him; but some doubted. Then Jesus came to them and said, "All authority in heaven and on earth has been given to me. Therefore go and make disciples of all nations, baptizing them in the name of the Father and of the Son and of the Holy Spirit, and teaching them to obey everything I have commanded you. And surely I am with you always, to the very end of the age." (Matthew 28:16-20)

Every Christian I know would say "yes and amen" to the Great Commission. They would even quote this scripture as part of their church or ministry objectives, but I do not see everyone obeying the first part of verse 20, 'teaching them to obey everything I have commanded you'.

This instruction of Jesus in the Book of Mark is consistent with Jesus' instruction in the rest of the Gospels. Jesus does not expect the Church to do anything He Himself did not do. For instance, about a third of Jesus' healing ministry was dedicated to 'driving out demons' in people's lives. He was teaching His disciples the principles of setting captives free from the hold the devil has over His people. Now, amongst many other instructions Jesus gave us, it is the responsibility of the Church of Jesus Christ.

> *He (Jesus) said to them, "Go into all the world and preach the good news to all creation. Whoever believes and is baptized will be saved, but whoever does not believe will be condemned. And these signs will accompany those who believe: In my name they will drive out demons; they will speak in new tongues; they will pick up snakes with their hands; and when they drink deadly poison, it will not hurt them at all; they will place their hands on sick people, and they will get well." After the Lord Jesus had spoken to them, he was taken up into heaven and he sat at the right hand of God. Then the disciples went out and preached everywhere, and the Lord worked with them and confirmed his word by the signs that accompanied it. (Mark 16:15-20)*

I know that many theological students would have an issue with the last part of Mark Chapter 16, because it was not included in the earlier manuscripts, but the teachings are consistent with the rest of the Gospels. I love that this passage of Scripture covers so much of Jesus' instruction to His Church, meaning every one of us, from Church leaders to the newly born-again Christian.

- He commands us to 'go'; get out and evangelize.
- He commands us to preach the good news to everyone.

- Whoever believes the message of the Gospel ought to be baptized.
- Signs and wonders will accompany those who believe and have faith that God will be there with them.
- Jesus' followers, meaning his true disciples, will drive out demons.
- They will speak in tongues.
- They will be protected – as Paul was when he was bitten by a viper, and everyone expected him to die (Acts 28:3-6). Even if unknowingly, they happen to drink poison, they will be protected.
- They will place their hands on the sick and they will get well.

We need to always remember, when we speak about 'Church', we are speaking about every individual who has given their life to Jesus. We are the Church of Jesus Christ. People often speak about the church as the building or the collective group of people who go to that building. But Church will always be me and you in God's Kingdom. So, God's plan is for us personally or collectively. An often-quoted verse from the Old Testament, which was originally in the context of the prophet Jeremiah writing a message to God's people, who were in exile in Babylon, shows God's heart towards His people.

> *"For I know the plans I have for you," declares the LORD, "plans to prosper you and not to harm you, plans to give you hope and a future."*
> *(Jeremiah 29:11)*

God has a plan for us and the Church as a whole. The enemy is trying to blind our eyes to this fact. He is terrified of us seeking and finding God's will. Don't worry what anyone says, seek the Lord with all your heart and you will find Him.

"You will seek me and find me when you seek me with all your heart. I will be found by you," declares the LORD, "and will bring you back from captivity." (Jeremiah 29:13-14)

He wants to give to us, His Church, the power of God that works through Jesus. In his letter to the Ephesians, the apostle Paul prays for the new Christian believers that they will get to know God better, because he wants them to have the Spirit of Wisdom and power.

For this reason, ever since I heard about your faith in the Lord Jesus and your love for all the saints, I have not stopped giving thanks for you, remembering you in my prayers. I keep asking that the God of our Lord Jesus Christ, the glorious Father, may give you the Spirit of wisdom and revelation, so that you may know him better. (Ephesians 1:15-17)

Paul continues with his prayer for them that the eyes of their heart would be enlightened to all that God has for them as part of Jesus' Church. These are exciting promises indeed.

I pray also that the eyes of your heart may be enlightened in order that you may know the hope to which he has called you, the riches of his glorious inheritance in the saints, and his incomparably great power for us who believe. That power is like the working of his mighty strength, which he exerted in Christ when he raised him from the dead and

seated him at his right hand in the heavenly realms.
(Ephesians 1:18-20)

The Role of the Local Church

What then is the role of the local church? Surely it is not intended to just be 'a bless me club' or a place where you can come, sing a few songs, and listen to messages which make you feel better, but where you are not challenged to do anything! What about putting God's word firmly into people's hearts, so they can consciously and deliberately bring change for the better?

I want to ask the question, "Did Jesus come to earth merely to save us for a trip to Heaven when we die?" No, definitely not! Why did Jesus appoint disciples? Was it just to establish church congregations around the world? I tell you the truth, Jesus came to establish His Church for us all to continue His work here on earth.

Sadly, I have to say I don't often see that happening. I see the deceiver, the father of lies, working hard to keep people deceived, offended, and critical of a loving heavenly Father God. That way he aims to make the Church look weak and irrelevant. I see the Church full of broken Christians who need healing but not many getting healed. The reason they are not, is because many churches do not operate in the full truth of the Word of God. Wrong teaching holds them back and, as a result, the people lack faith and are unable to trust in the Lord.

As we read the four Gospels, Matthew, Mark, Luke and John, we learn about all the things Jesus did. And as He was doing all these amazing miracles, preaching the Good News, the people were believing in Him, putting their faith in Him and receiving Him as Lord of their lives. Because they believed, people everywhere were being healed of sickness and disease, and many were set free from demonic intrusion. This is what Jesus trained His disciples to do, so that, after His death, they could carry on doing what He did. What we learn about the disciples of Jesus' day should apply to the Church today. Every Christian is part of the Church. God is speaking to every one of us.

The Jesus Model of Church

Jesus knew, once He entered His public ministry, He would not have that much time to equip His disciples before His death. He did not seem to teach the disciples any methodology. Rather, He took them with Him, and they learned on the job. If we are looking for a method for ministry, we are way off track. At Ellel Ministries we have adopted Luke 9:11 for our focus guideline.

He (Jesus) welcomed them and spoke to them about the kingdom of God, and healed those who needed healing. (Luke 9:11)

So, our focus is welcoming, teaching the Kingdom of God and healing people. This is God's ministry, and our team are servants in His Kingdom. He has given us His Holy Spirit to lead, and we are just the facilitators of what we sense the Spirit of God is saying the course of prayer ministry should be. We dare not rely on a method. All we must do is to try and understand how Jesus taught His disciples. We can learn the principles we need to follow from that.

Jesus welcomed the people, and we try make the people feel as welcome as we can when they are with us. Jesus taught the people about the Kingdom of God. We teach the people about the Kingdom of God – not the kingdom of the Church. Jesus healed people in various ways. God has taught us, and we are still learning, what makes people ill and causes them to be out of God's blessing. We do this by asking God what's on His heart and how the Holy Spirit wants to lead in bringing healing to God's people. There is no method, no technique and definitely not a six-session-fix-it program. This is Holy Spirit ministry.

Jesus prepared and equipped His disciples well. What the disciples were learning was completely strange to them, completely new and totally amazing. Whatever Jesus taught touched their hearts, something no other teacher was able to do while teaching the Law. What the disciples were learning was straight from the heart of God.

Jesus taught the importance of love and acceptance, forgiving each other, confessing, repenting, faithfulness, good attitude, and so much more. But the most important thing of all was that Jesus revealed His Father to each one of the disciples and us. We learn that God the Father loves us and has a plan and a purpose for us all.

Jesus understands that we were all in the kingdom of darkness, some for a longer time than others. Our backgrounds vary, and so the damage to our emotions, the state of mind, our human spirit, soul and body have all been different. Some have given the enemy footholds in their lives which need to be removed. But the Holy Spirit knows how to gently and lovingly lead us in the way Jesus would bring healing.

This is His Holy Spirit ministry. He does not want to embarrass anyone. We have worked hard for our Ellel Centers to be safe places for people to come to without feeling exposed. One thing you can't do is shock us with your past. No matter what your past has been, it can be forgiven and cleansed by the blood of the Lamb.

The Amazing Reality of Luke Nine

Due to the fall, Adam and Eve lost their relationship with God as well as the permission to operate in God's power and authority. Satan deceived them and usurped their authority to rule and reign on earth. This situation lasted throughout the ages until we get to Luke Chapter nine when Jesus restores to us, His Church, what Adam and Eve lost.

Jesus had spent His years in public ministry teaching His disciples, healing them of past hurts and equipping them for His work on earth. It was time to commission His small group of faithful followers and make them into a dynamic ministry team. Jesus then restored to His Church the power and authority Adam and Eve lost in the garden through disobedience to God. This is vital to the Church.

When Jesus had called the Twelve together, he gave them power and authority to drive out all demons and to cure diseases, and he sent them out to preach the kingdom of God and to heal the sick. (Luke 9:1-2)

Now that power and authority had been given, Jesus, the 'last' or 'second' Adam, left the disciples with four major obligations which would be necessary for His Church to be successful in this dark world. He had majored on these four areas throughout His ministry. He sent His disciples out to put into practice all that He taught them. Their ministry would not be limited to any one particular location, such as a synagogue or a temple. Does that mean that today we should be thinking of Kingdom activities outside the walls of our church building?

So they (the disciples) set out and went from village to village, preaching the gospel and healing people everywhere (Luke 9:6)

From this scripture I draw four major focus points for the ministry of the Church today.
1. Drive out *all* demons
2. Cure diseases
3. Preach the Kingdom of God
4. Heal the sick

In local churches around the world today, generally speaking, which of the four focus points are regularly operational? I would say only number three. Even then, it's not always preaching about the Kingdom of God, but can often be more about preaching 'the kingdom of this church', with its particular emphasis and culture.

What about the other three focus points? What theology have we invented not to do them, if they are what Jesus instructed His Church to do? Are our eyes closed to the Scriptures and the commands of Jesus Christ? How can we be the powerful Church Jesus intended us to be when we are not driving out demons; curing diseases; preaching the Kingdom of God and healing the sick?

Eyes Closed Again?

I have had many discussions with leaders who tell me they don't believe in 'driving out demons'. Many others don't want to talk about it at all and it seems to be a closed book for them. Maybe it is that their eyes are opened to parts of the Gospel but closed to other parts. How are we living out the Gospel when we are not obeying God instructions? I wonder if we should even call ourselves the Church of Jesus Christ, if we do not preach His word in its fullness. If we don't, we are a church of half the Gospel, and maybe even less.

> *For though we live in the world, we do not wage war as the world does. The weapons we fight with are not the weapons of the world. On the contrary, they have divine power to demolish strongholds. We demolish arguments and every pretension that sets itself up against the knowledge of God, and we take captive every thought to make it obedient to Christ. And we will be ready to punish every act of disobedience, once your obedience is complete. (2 Corinthians 10:3-6)*

I have often attempted to teach truth about the healing ministry of Jesus to Christians, only to find that they reject it and cannot receive it. Even when they have read what is clearly written in their own Bible, they have said to me, "But my church does not teach that." Does this mean that we can regard the practices of our church as better than the instructions God gave to His Church?

I am reminded of a distraught father who brought his son to the disciples for healing but found they could not heal him. So, he took his son directly to Jesus, who delivered the boy.

The rebuke that Jesus spoke to His disciples was pretty severe. If He described them as an 'unbelieving and perverse generation' after they were unsuccessful in their attempt to bring healing and deliverance to the desperate man's son, I wonder what words He would use to address those parts of His Church today who don't even try.

"O unbelieving and perverse generation," Jesus replied, "how long shall I stay with you? How long shall I put up with you? Bring the boy here to me." Jesus rebuked the demon, and it came out of the boy, and he was healed from that moment. Then the disciples came to Jesus in private and asked, "Why couldn't we drive it out?" He replied, "Because you have so little faith. I tell you the truth, if you have faith as small as a mustard seed, you can say to this mountain, 'Move from here to there' and it will move. Nothing will be impossible for you.'" (Matthew 17:17-20)

Nothing is impossible for the radically passionate Christian whose faith is in Jesus. It's not too late to make right with God and crawl out of our shells, be equipped and stand tall for Jesus, doing His work in this dark world.

Church Leaders Should Have Integrity

Beryl and I were pastors for twelve glorious years and so we know what church life is all about. To be working on a pastoral team is the best, but sometimes the toughest, place on earth to be. It is the best place to be, because when everything is going well, the experience of a loving Christian environment is unbeatable on earth. It is also the toughest place to be, because expectations are so high.

From our own personal experience, we know the challenges for leaders in church life, the pain, the hurt and sometimes the trauma of betrayal. From ministering to many leaders and pastors, we know that the enemy will use the constant pressure and unhealed areas of their lives to tempt them into sin and hence undermine their ministry.

But also, from our experience, we have seen how the healing power of Jesus can bring restoration and renewed vision, when they are willing to humble themselves and receive ministry. After all, Jesus came to restore the heart of man to the heart of God. This makes us passionate to see people healed and restored to continue in service to the King. But we are sad when we see the Body of Christ missing out on the blessing God has for His people because some leaders fail to address their sinful issues and try to live a double life.

We know that Jesus will one day judge all things because He is the judge. The Bible is our instruction book for life, guidance, correction and discipline. We would benefit hugely to be mindful of every word that Jesus taught as well as the principles of the Old Testament. I once heard Derek Prince, a world-renowned Bible teacher, say (slightly paraphrased); *"Let us not judge the Bible by the Church, but let us judge the Church by the Bible"*.

What wisdom! Remember, the Church is made up of repentant sinners. Now that's God's grace!

As a pastor, it is necessary to be on your guard all the time with what you say and how you say it, and what you do and how you do it. Pastors have both a public and a private life, but it would be totally wrong to completely separate them out from one another. How I behave at home should reflect my calling as a pastor in the church.

In my travels around Africa and aboard, I find that many Christians separate their church life from their secular life. The way they live their church life is holy, but the way they - leaders and members alike - live their private lives has nothing to do with church, so they reckon that they can do life as they wish.

How can I ever forget the day I was teaching in one church on the subject of sexuality? After the teaching, during a time of corporate ministry, the leader stood up and accused his fellow ministers of being spiritual prostitutes. He accused them of taking advantage of widows and single mothers by having sex with them as a reward for praying for them. I was shocked that such behavior was prevalent amongst those who are looked up to as leaders and teachers.

Leaders in the Church Should be Equippers

I believe God is looking for churches, who are raising up disciples to do the work of Jesus on earth by setting captives free. I believe God will see that kind of church as a successful church, led by a successful leader. God will not be looking to see how many people we have gathered to attend our church services, but the effectiveness of the members in continuing the work of Jesus on earth.

If church leaders do not teach the whole truth by teaching and equipping their people to be effective witnesses for Christ, they are failing in their calling and mandate, which says, *'until we all* reach *unity in the faith and in the knowledge of the Son of God and become mature, attaining to the whole*

measure of the fullness of Christ.' It is the church leaders'
role to ensure they use the various giftings of members in the
wider Body of Christ to equip the saints for service.

> *It was he who gave some to be apostles, some to be
> prophets, some to be evangelists, and some to be
> pastors and teachers to <u>prepare God's people for
> works of service</u>, so that the body of Christ may be
> built up until we all reach unity in the faith and in
> the knowledge of the Son of God and become
> mature, attaining to the whole measure of the
> fullness of Christ. (Ephesians 4:11-13)*

Failing to 'prepare God's people for works of service' is
failing in obedience to God's call as a church leader. A
spiritually weak leader may be the reason why a church is not
reflecting the life of Christ and the spiritual gifts of the Holy
Spirit. The church may be full of strong personalities, but
they lack the power of the Holy Spirit in their lives. Ezekiel
34 is a good chapter for shepherds to read.

Paul spells out in Ephesians 4:11 who should be doing the
equipping. This is normally known as 'the Fivefold
Ministry'. I must add that, those called and anointed to equip
others don't necessarily have to be the full-time leaders in the
church. Those who are called and anointed to equip God's
people in works of service should be released to do so.

Often, the equipping and experiences one has in the world
will be used by God for His Kingdom. However, without the
working of the Holy Spirit in the life of the trainer, the
training will remain worldly. No matter how 'good'
preaching or teaching may seem, it cannot be said to be

inspired by the Holy Spirit, if the Holy Spirit is not at work in the life of the speaker.

The Church Should be a Safe Place

Unfortunately, the Church may not have proven to be the safest of places. Harsh domination, manipulation, intimidation and even total rejection may have been the response of leadership in dealing with people needing restoration. When I get the opportunity to preach, I always look for the opportunity to encourage Christians to make their church a place where people from the community can safely go for help.

We, as individuals, are the Church that Jesus is coming back for, and that Church is you and me, not the church building. So, when I say, "Let's make the church a safe place", I mean we need to be safe people in our local church where people can find someone to confide in.

We have tried to do this at our Centre by creating an atmosphere in which it is easier, even for our team members, to raise and deal with any issues that may arise. We have done this by much prayer and spiritual cleansing of our property. We are able to speak to each other about our weaknesses, because we understand we all have come out of a place of brokenness and we all need healing, even today.

We are all a 'work in progress', individuals living in a fallen world and in need of healing. We even call ourselves 'wounded' healers. Wounded, yes, like everyone else, who has the courage to admit it, but healed enough to serve the King of kings and the Lord of lords. This, I believe, is a goal the Church of Jesus needs to strive for.

Probably one of the most devastating hindrances for blocking the move of the Holy Spirit is gossip. No one admits to gossip, but it seems many people in the church gossip. The one listening to gossip is as guilty as the one gossiping. It seems we love letting others know what we know.

A gossip betrays a confidence; so avoid a man who talks too much. (Proverbs 20:19)

Paul puts gossip on the same level of sin issues as debauchery or wickedness.

For I (Paul) am afraid that when I come I may not find you as I want you to be, and you may not find me as you want me to be. I fear that there may be quarrelling, jealousy, outbursts of anger, factions (holy huddles), slander, gossip, arrogance and disorder. I am afraid that when I come again my God will humble me before you, and I will be grieved over many who have sinned earlier and have not repented of the impurity, sexual sin and debauchery in which they have indulged. (2Corinthians 12:20-21)

Gossip is serious stuff and is frowned upon by God. When I recognize it, I stop it and remove it from our teams. How can holiness ever be part of our ministry with this stuff being tolerated? Sorry for the straight talk. If someone wants to gossip to you about an issue they have with another person, the minute you realize a gossip story is coming, you should stop them in their tracks, and offer them help. The Bible says,

if you are offering your gift at the altar and there remember that your brother has something against

you, leave your gift there in front of the altar. First
go and be reconciled to your brother; then come and
offer your gift. Settle matters quickly with your
adversary. (Matthew 5:23-25)

So, offer to pray for the gossipers and encourage them to
make things right, to forgive or ask for forgiveness from the
person they are gossiping about.

Are we Building God's Kingdom?

(Jesus said) "I will give you the keys of the kingdom
of heaven; whatever you bind on earth will be bound
in heaven, and whatever you loose on earth will be
loosed in heaven." (Matthew 16:19)

Jesus said these words in relation to building His Church. In
order to do His work on earth, He will give us the keys to do
so. But it often seems that much of the Church just want to
preach week in and week out, never equipping or releasing
the saints into effective ministry. Is this why the Church has
no voice today? Is this why the Church is not effective in the
marketplace?

Are we guilty of building the kingdom of the church as
opposed to building the Kingdom of God? It's never been
about the kingdom of the church, but always about the
Kingdom of God. He will give us, the Church, the authority
to bind and loose, to push back the kingdom of darkness and
set the captives free. The Kingdom of God will increase and
be loosed on the earth as we make disciples who are truly
following Jesus and learning to do the things He did.

If we, as the Church, are building the wrong kingdom,
however, darkness will reign. Darkness comes in at that place

of unbelief, where the Church of Jesus Christ tries to achieve the same things that the world desires, such as status, success and recognition.

> *I beg you that when I come I may not have to be as bold as I expect to be toward some people who think that we live by the standards of this world. (2 Corinthians 10:2)*

The Church Should be a Spiritual Hospital

God wants to see us healed and free of the bondages, pain, wounds, shame, disappointments, abuse and sin issues in our life. These deep issues can only be dealt with in the Kingdom of God with help of the Holy Spirit. This is the role of the Church.

> *When Jesus had called the Twelve together, he gave them power and authority to drive out all demons and to cure diseases, and he sent them out to preach the kingdom of God and to heal the sick. (Luke 9:1-2)*

A church in God's Kingdom, which is failing to continue the work of Jesus on earth, is falling short of the mandate of her calling. A church, not setting captives free and healing the sick, is not using the power and authority, which Jesus gave to His Church.

We were invited to take a team to minister at a lovely church in a rural town. The church was very highly thought of in the community. Being in the healing ministry for many years and a pastor for twelve years, my heart was to see the church discipled, which includes healing the wounds of the past and equipping other Christians to do the same. It was because of the focus of our ministry that we were invited to minister and introduce the healing ministry of Jesus to their members. We happily taught and ministered in healing prayer to people for two days. However, there were so many people wanting personal ministry that we could not pray for them all in the allocated time.

Moments before departing for the journey home, we noticed something appeared to be wrong. When we asked if anything was wrong, the pastor's wife complained that we had left them with a pile of ministry needs to attend to. This was not quite the response we were hoping for. In hindsight, I have to agree with her because, contrary to what she expected, there was still a lot of work to be done. However, I remembered a remark she had made when we arrived about what a mature, active and loving congregation they had.

Again, I have to agree with her observation, as they really were amazing people. They were lovely people, but I know they were deeply hurting inside, with no place to go. The pastoral couple had told their people so often about how wonderful they were and how mature they were in handling life's issues that the congregation did not want to disappoint them. So, they had stuffed everything down into their 'emotional basement' and put a tight lid on it. When we came along and taught on God's heart for healing, the emotional lid just exploded.

I think what we learned from this experience is that a true shepherd's heart should be focused on trying to care for his flock individually. If that is too difficult to do for some reason, the shepherd should work towards appropriately equipping a prayer and counselling ministry team to assist in the vital function of caring for the individual emotional needs of the flock.

Breakthrough in Rwanda

The need for the church to be a spiritual hospital was so clearly shown during an amazing mission trip we had to Rwanda in 2009. We were invited to teach and minister at a five-day conference in Kigali, the capital of Rwanda. Ellel teams from South Africa and England came for this vital event. The then Archbishop Kolini of the Anglican Church was our VIP guest. There were about 160 attendees, most of them pastors and senior leaders. Most of our guests could not speak English, so an interpreter was needed. A lovely young man named Lambert offered his services and what a great job he did.

Another guest who had previously visited Ellel Grange in the north of England had received amazing healing. Her testimony is incredible. In short, during the genocide, the Hutu militia had attacked the Tutsi village where she lived and just about wiped out the whole village. She was fourteen years old at the time.

She was hit over the head with a machete and, thinking she was dead, they threw her into a mass grave. She was later rescued by surviving villagers to tell the tale. However, she suffered unbearable headaches and constant nightmares as a result. During her ministry at Ellel Grange, the pain in her memory, the trauma she was still suffering, and her head pains were completely healed. God did an awesome work.

She was asked to share her testimony with the conference guests. Try and picture the scene at the conference. Without us realizing it would happen, the one hundred and sixty guests were a mixture of Hutus and Tutsis. Victims, as well as people whose family members had been perpetrators, were gathered together in one venue. Here was a Tutsi lady giving her testimony and a young Hutu man interpreting the gory details of what happened to her during the genocide. It was a long testimony, and you could feel the atmosphere thickening as her story unfolded.

I and the whole team were so engrossed in her story that we almost forgot to pray. Then some of us realized the truth of the situation and began to pray. How we prayed! All of a sudden, Lambert, our young Hutu interpreter fell on his knees before this Tutsi lady and asked her, on behalf of the Hutu tribe, to forgive them. God's presence fell on everyone there. His presence was so tangible tears throughout the auditorium flowed.

All the Hutus were on their knees under the conviction of the Holy Spirit, asking for forgiveness. Tutsis were crying as they were forgiving the Hutu countrymen and women. Our team were so relieved God showed up and defused a potentially volatile situation. Testimonies of forgiveness, healing and a new sense of freedom flowed from the conference guests. This same young interpreter now plays a major role of bringing healing to his nation in Rwanda.

Lambert's Story

This is Lambert's testimony.

'Growing up in a village in the Southwest of Rwanda, I considered myself one of the few privileged and fortunate. Both my mum and dad had jobs and were well regarded in the village. However, despite all this, life threw a lot of challenges and difficulties at me which brought pain and hurt in my life. I struggled with this into adulthood, when I met Jesus, the healer and bearer of our pain. Although outwardly I was progressing well in school and ascending the social ladder, I was full of bitterness, hatred, anger, mistrust, suspicion, shame, and despair.

Conceived as a surprise to both of my parents, I had become a source of contention before I was even born. My parents were not prepared for a third child, and especially not a third boy. To complicate the matter, I grew up shy and quiet in contrast to my two older brothers. Each time I was compared to one or both of them, it reinforced my sense of inadequacy and insecurity. By the time the genocide against the Tutsis happened in 1994, I was a broken thirteen-year-old, just starting to try to understand myself and my place in the world around me.

I fled the country to Congo (DRC, called Zaire at that time) and had to grow up as quickly as possible in a refugee camp where most social structures were lacking. Sometimes I look back and wonder where my teenage years went. Later, another war broke out in Congo, and so I returned to Rwanda, with no future prospects, other than now being able to die on my ancestral soil. I was without a home, and full of bitterness, shame, and hopelessness.

Two years later I came to the Lord, in 1998. It was a turning point in my life where I left the life of sin behind and started pursuing God with diligence. Unfortunately, though I was full of joy to know that my sins were forgiven, I continued to live a life of suspicion, hatred, division, bitterness, and sorrow. Though I was praising God, and serving him as much as I could, my life was still full of pain, confusion, striving and prejudice.

I have discovered that Jesus did not die for my sin alone, but also for my sorrow, grief, and pain. This has been transforming in my life and set me on a journey of understanding more about God's love for me, who I am in Him and how to live life with a sense of destiny. It started with the healing of ethnic wounds.

After sharing my pain, sorrow, and grief about how the events of the genocide against Tutsis affected me and my family, I discovered that we are all created in His image and for His glory. God gave me love for everybody and a passion to help others be healed and restored.

Later on, Ellel South Africa came to Rwanda and held a five-day teaching and healing conference. I was asked to be the interpreter from English into my local Kinyarwanda language. During this conference, Jesus lifted from me the shame I had carried for years from what 'my people' had done in the genocide.

Jesus helped me to forgive my own people and to stand in the gap for their sins. Then He took me back to my early life and healed the rejection I experienced growing up. This brought a sense of peace, purpose, identity, and security which I had never experienced before. I shifted from slaving for God's love and approval to serving as a son in my Father's vineyard. My heart now is to see others healed and restored, so that they can fulfil God's purpose in their lives.

Although I had been born again, I still had inner pain. But God came, in His perfect timing, and healed me on the inside. Now I am delivered. I am free indeed, and day by day I am His work in progress, as I draw closer and closer to Him. Today, by God's grace, I am serving the Lord in Ellel Ministries, the amazing ministry which showed me the keys to my healing. Ellel Ministries is now established in Rwanda, teaching and bringing the good news of God's healing power to my fellow Rwandans in the precious name of Jesus.

I wish someone had told me back in 1998 that the Jesus I invited into my heart was not only my sin-bearer, but also my pain-bearer. It would have saved me years of slaving for God's love, and causing heartache to the people around me through my anger, harshness, and lack of compassion. May all believers get to meet Him fully, not just part of Him. I am now healed, equipped and anointed to heal the broken-hearted (Isaiah 61:1).'

A Cry for Help

It would do the whole Rwandan story injustice if I left out what happened at the end of the Kigali conference. Normally, a dignitary such as the Archbishop would be invited to open the conference with a word and in prayer, and return for the final session for a closing prayer. However, the Archbishop sat through the whole five-day conference and his concluding words deeply impacted me and the whole Ellel Ministries team. He said, "Now I understand that we are a traumatized Church trying to heal a traumatized nation. Will you please come and help us?" As a result, a couple of years later, Ellel Ministries was established in Rwanda. Today, we are bringing healing and equipping to the Rwandan people on a daily basis.

In this chapter we have been exploring God's plan for the Church which should be the expression of His Kingdom here on earth. In the next chapter we will look at how our lives should be different when our eyes are opened, and we come out of the darkness and start to live in His Kingdom.

Chapter 5
Living in the Light

Receiving Jesus as my personal Lord and Savior was an awesome experience. There was a change that took place inside me that's difficult to explain. I definitely sensed a strong emotional feeling, a feeling that something had happened inside of me. I felt I was forgiven, but I knew I needed to be cleaner. Then I learnt it was by grace I was saved through my faith in Christ and not by anything I had done.

> *For it is by grace you have been saved, through faith—and this not from yourselves, it is the gift of God — not by works, so that no one can boast. (Ephesians 2:8-9)*

The incredible thing is, God chose me and renewed my spirit. The realization that God chose me, that Jesus died for me and that He had a personal interest in me changed my life. This gift of life is available for everyone who chooses to receive Jesus as Lord of their lives. I am now a child of God in His Kingdom. Because I am now in Jesus and Jesus is in me, provided I live life God's way on earth, I have everlasting life, that is, life after death. Heaven is my new destination.

> *"Because I live, you also will live." (John 14:19b)*

I now find I want to live life being part of the solution and no longer part of the problem.

I can just imagine the Ephesians receiving the Gospel teachings from Paul, the awe, the excitement, as the Holy Spirit spoke deep into their thirsty spirits as He did in me.

Looking back at my life, I realize I was coming out of a life of darkness, without Jesus in my heart. There was actually no light, just darkness. My life was empty with no meaning. Jesus brought light into my life, and now I have been healed of my past. I guard that light with everything I have. These scriptures spoke deep into my heart and gave me understanding.

> *When Jesus spoke again to the people, he said, "I am the light of the world. Whoever follows me will never walk in darkness, but will have the light of life." (John 8:12)*

When darkness reigns in our lives, there is no light.

An extraordinary thing happened to me as I was writing this book on the topic of *'Eyes Opened, Eyes Closed'*. I found that I was struggling to focus on the words I was typing. I went to my optometrist friend, whom I had not visited for some years, thinking my reading glasses needed replacing. After testing my eyes, he informed me that my eyes were at an advanced stage of Cataracts. So, off I went to the Eye Clinic for further tests, only to be told that, not only did the Cataracts need removing, but I also needed the lenses in my eyes replaced.

Thank the Lord for medical science! Now, after having had those procedures, I have 20/20 vision. In fact, after I had read the various sized letters on his surgery wall chart, the surgeon said that I had 'eagle' vision. I was really happy about that. Medical science can remove darkness with a physical cause, such as, in my case, the aging process. But science cannot remove darkness in our soul. Only Jesus can do that. Even if we are physically blind, Jesus can bring light into our soul through the born-again process.

"The eye is the lamp of the body. If your eyes are good, your whole body will be full of light. But if your eyes are bad, your whole body will be full of darkness. If then the light within you is darkness, how great is that darkness! (Matthew 6:22-23)

It is so important for us to recognize and understand that whether we have light or darkness within us depends upon whether our spiritual eyes are open or closed. We need to ask ourselves, "are my spiritual eyes open or closed?" Not all leaders help to keep our spiritual eyes open. If we are not spiritually aware enough, our eyes can be slowly and subtly closed through false teaching. This permits darkness to flow back into our lives.

Jesus spoke to his faithful followers, announcing to them that they were light carriers in His Kingdom. This also applies to us today. Whoever takes the Word and works of Jesus into the marketplace carries His light into a dark world. With Jesus in us, we are now the light of the world. What an awesome honor!

"You are the light of the world. (Matthew 5:14)

To be a light carrier for Jesus, we need to live the best way we can, not allowing His light in us to dim in any way. If we are now the *'light of the world'*, I'm sure Jesus did not mean us to hide our light away when we walk out the door of our home into the world. He wants us to shine, be kind to people, helpful, courteous, encouraging, and ready for anything. He wants us to do this outside the walls of our home. Although the world is a 'dark' place, He still loves the people living there, and He relies on us to be His light.

For God so loved the world that he gave his one and only Son, that whoever believes in him shall not perish but have eternal life (John 3:16)

What a privilege to be a carrier of good news into darkness to the ones He loves!

Living in Darkness

Unfortunately, people chose not to recognize who Jesus was. Still, today, people do not want to recognize who Jesus really is. When Paul refers to *'this dark world'*, he is referring to those people not yet choosing to live a life in the Light of God the Father and with Jesus Christ as their Savior and Redeemer, but choosing to remain in *'this dark world'*.

He (Jesus) was in the world, and though the world was made through him, the world did not recognize him. He came to that which was his own, but his own did not receive him. Yet to all who received him, to those who believed in his name, he gave the right to become children of God— children born not of natural descent, nor of human decision or a husband's will, but born of God. (John 1:10-13)

In Paul's letter to the Ephesians, Paul explains that there is a spiritual battle and it's not against flesh and blood (Ephesians 6:12). The spiritual battle in the heavenlies is about capturing the souls of men and women on earth. The battle is largely for our free will. Unfortunately, many Christians, due to the lack of discipleship available in the Church today, live a mixture of disobedience and obedience to Jesus, but it does not work. There is no faithfulness in a life of mixture. If we are against God's will, we are surrendering to Satan. There is an inevitable clash. Paul explains that there are two elements at war against God and his Christian followers in the kingdom of darkness.

For our struggle is not against flesh and blood, but against the rulers, against the authorities, against the powers of this dark world and against the spiritual forces of evil in the heavenly realms. (Ephesians 6:12)

There are the powers of *'this dark world'* (meaning those on earth doing Satan's will) and *'the spiritual forces of evil in the heavenly realm'* (meaning the demonic realm) that have ganged up together to hate all that God stands for. Because they are against God, they are against Christians. Jesus warned us this would happen. Living a life of mixture makes us neither hot nor cold. We will have neither total light nor total darkness. Our eyes are neither fully open nor fully closed. Jesus gave a strong rebuke to Christians living like that in Revelation Chapter 3.

So, because you are lukewarm—neither hot nor cold—I am about to spit you out of my mouth. You say, 'I am rich; I have acquired wealth and do not need a thing.' But you do not realize that you are wretched, pitiful, poor, blind and naked. I counsel you to buy from me gold refined in the fire, so you can become rich; and white clothes to wear, so you can cover your shameful nakedness; and salve to put on your eyes, so you can see. (Revelation 3:16-18)

Born-again Christians, also called children of God, live physically in the world but are anchored spiritually in the Kingdom of God. They are sure of their eternal destiny.

Many people, who have not committed their lives to Jesus, will say things like, "I've lived a good life", or "The man upstairs will let me in", but they are living with false hopes. Jesus invites us to believe in Him like a little child and to receive Him as our personal Savior. His invitation to us to do that is the only guarantee of salvation. The key word in the following scripture is 'humility', and the most frightening statement in the same scripture is that, unless we change, we will never enter the Kingdom of God.

> *He called a little child and had him stand among them. And he said: "I tell you the truth, unless you change and become like little children, you will never enter the kingdom of heaven. Therefore, whoever humbles himself like this child is the greatest in the kingdom of heaven." (Matthew 18:2-4)*

These are not difficult words to understand. All those of us who are in the Kingdom of God, at one time had to humble ourselves, bow our knee to Jesus, the only living God, ask for forgiveness of our sins and receive Him as Lord. We had to ask Him to come into our hearts and make us new. This was our second birth.

This is how every one of us enters the Kingdom of God. Our eyes can then be opened to truth, enabling us to deal with the consequences of our past, through the work of the Holy Spirit, the Counsellor. Once our eyes are spiritually wide open, we read the Gospels as a priority, so that we can get close to Jesus and hear His heart for us. If the desires of our heart are in line with His will, He will give us what we desire – in His perfect timing.

*Delight yourself in the LORD and he will give you
the desires of your heart. (Psalm 37:4)*

There will always be a condition to a promise. In this case it
is *'delight yourself in the Lord'*. When we are in that right
relationship with Him, He gives us our heart's desire, if it's
in line with His will. He always knows what is best for us.

God Loves the World

In the Bible the world is referred to as Satan's domain, where
Satan is the prince.

*"Now is the time for judgment on this world; now
the prince of this world will be driven out. But I,
when I am lifted up from the earth, will draw all men
to myself." (John 12:31-32)*

God our Father loves the world. If you are a child of God,
saved by the blood of Jesus and you have bowed your knee
to receive Him as Lord of your life, God has spiritually
translated you out of the world into His Kingdom. Every
Christian was at one stage of their lives in Satan's kingdom
of darkness.

Let's not point fingers at the world because of what they are
doing or saying against Christians or Jesus. Ask yourself
what you can do to show them a better place, to show them
the Kingdom of God. Because God loves the world, we too
need to love the world with the same agape love as He does.
The only difference between the world and the Christian is
the cross. When Jesus prays for His disciples in John Chapter
17, He is praying to the Father and teaching us at the same
time. Here is Jesus praying to God the Father:

"I have revealed you to those whom you gave me out
of the world. They were yours; you gave them to me
and they have obeyed your word." (John 17:6)

Jesus revealed Father God to us through His preaching and
the miracles He performed. God gives all those who have
faith in Him to Jesus, because they obey His Word. Now that
we have said "Yes" to Jesus, He redeems us out of the world,
and we become born again by the Spirit of God.

We begin the journey of learning how to become obedient,
no longer doing what the world does. Our true healing starts
at salvation. The closer we get to God, and the more we
become obedient, the more our light will shine before others.

You may want to ask the question, "Does God only choose
certain people?" No, He does not. God loves everyone and
He speaks to everyone in different ways, but not everyone
listens. I remember times when I would hear a sermon on the
radio, and quickly move on to the next station. Maybe God
wanted me to listen a little longer, because He wanted to use
the speakers' voice to speak to me. But I chose not to listen.

Snatched from the Fire

The moment we humble ourselves and give our hearts to
Jesus and make Him Lord of our lives, He immediately
snatches us out of the kingdom of darkness and transports us
spiritually into his Kingdom. Here is a scripture which I find
most encouraging and exciting. I realize the Scriptures are
always relevant, some for now, others for a time to come.
Since I gave my heart to Jesus, Scripture reading has come
alive in my spirit. This is an extract from Jude's hard-hitting
letter which had such a profound impact on my life:

But, dear friends, remember what the apostles of our Lord Jesus Christ foretold. They said to you, "In the last times there will be scoffers who will follow their own ungodly desires." These are the men who divide you, who follow mere natural instincts and do not have the Spirit. But you, dear friends, build yourselves up in your most holy faith and pray in the Holy Spirit. Keep yourselves in God's love as you wait for the mercy of our Lord Jesus Christ to bring you to eternal life. Be merciful to those who doubt; snatch others from the fire and save them; to others show mercy, mixed with fear—hating even the clothing stained by corrupted flesh. (Jude:17-23)

I was snatched from the fire for sure. Now Jude encourages us to *'snatch others from the fire'*. As I was snatched from the fire, I too should snatch others from the fire, but I see so many taking the easier way. Once saved, they sit back and couldn't care a hoot about those around them on the slippery slope to Hell. We need to always be proactive in revealing Jesus to others, even if it's merely through our godly lifestyle.

I have learned that hard-hitting evangelism is not the only way to rescue people for Jesus. The softer approach of friendship, kindness, speaking good of others and giving genuine encouragement are also extremely effective ways in showing people an alternative way of life.

I remember, some years ago, I attended a pastors' conference near Peterborough in the UK. During a lunch break, a group of us were talking and getting to know each other. One pastor was speaking about a situation he was having with his son who seemed to be struggling to receive the Lord as his Savior.

He had been lovingly ministering to his son, and his son was open to receive but did not know how to make a commitment to the Lord. The pastor, after witnessing to his son, encouraged him on a number of occasions to go up to his room, close the door and ask Jesus into his life. But, he said, it did not seem to work. I could sense his despair.

Being a bit of an evangelist myself, I asked him what he did for a living before he became a pastor. His answer was perfect. He said he was a motorcar salesman. I could feel the stares I got from the other pastors in the group. Here was a man speaking about an intimate situation about his son and here I was asking a question that seemed totally irrelevant. I had to pluck up a lot of courage to continue.

My next question to him was, "If you were a salesman, you would know how to close a deal." He affirmed that he did. I then asked him why he didn't close the deal with his son as he would close a deal on a car sale. 'What do you mean?" he asked. The other British pastors listened intently to see where I was going with this. "Well!", I said, "If your son is so keen to receive the Lord, and is obviously not sure how, ask the golden question."

"What question is that?" he asked, a little surprised. He did not know where I was going with this. "Ask your son if he would like to receive the Lord Jesus as his Savior," I replied, hoping he would not mind me using a secular technique to get a spiritual conclusion. I continued, "He is obviously going to say yes. When he does, ask him if he would like to repeat a sinner's prayer after you and invite Jesus into his heart".

The penny finally dropped, not only for the dad, but also everyone in the group. There was a big "Ahaa!" from all the other pastors. I was so relieved that my explanation went so well. Sometimes, we want to be so polite, not wanting to offend. Evangelism, even if it is done as gently as a dove, is powerful. It's letting your light shine in the darkness. No matter how you snatch people out of darkness, be Jesus 'in the flesh', so to speak, to them. Speak to and treat others as Jesus would. He loves us to be His hands and feet here on earth.

Christians Should be Different

Should you happen to be in the presence of a person who is not yet saved, realize that darkness still reigns in that person's life. See this as a God-inspired moment of opportunity. With the light of life shining in you, be a channel of Jesus' love for the unlovable, accepting the person, but never the sin. You are a light in their dark space. God may want to use you. People may not understand they are seeing your light, but they will see you as pleasantly and refreshingly 'different'.

I love this scripture in Isaiah.

> *Arise, shine, for your light has come, and the glory of the LORD rises upon you. See, darkness covers the earth and thick darkness is over the peoples, but the LORD rises upon you and his glory appears over you. (Isiah 60:1-2)*

Although Isaiah was referring to the coming Messiah, Jesus confirms that the light He has is also in us.

In the same way, let your light shine before men, that they may see your good deeds and praise your Father in heaven. (Matthew 5:16)

Here is an invitation from Jesus Himself.

When Jesus spoke again to the people, he said, "I am the light of the world. Whoever follows me will never walk in darkness, but will have the light of life." (John 8:12)

Paul explains here that those walking in the righteousness of God reflect the Lord's glory.

And we, who with unveiled faces all reflect the Lord's glory, are being transformed into his likeness with ever-increasing glory, which comes from the Lord, who is the Spirit. (2 Corinthians 3:18)

When on holiday, we frequently visit a resort village at the coast. Our neighbor in the cottage next to us is a man who is not well liked in the village, because of his deceitful, untrustworthy character. Knowing the situation, and also well aware that he was living in sin and in a dark place in his life, I saw this as an opportunity to make a difference in his life. Because I treated him with respect and was prepared to talk with him, he always seeks me out for conversation.

He now knows I'm a Christian and often turns the conversation to religion, and I find that can be a minefield for disagreement and arguments. Whenever he swears, I tell him I don't appreciate his language. Whenever he wants to gossip or tell me an unsavory joke, I tell him I don't want to hear it. But I do receive him enthusiastically. He now knows my boundaries and the no-go areas with me.

One evening, out of the blue, he came to visit and told me his life's story and that he wanted to change. I shared the Gospel and how to be saved. But when it came to counting the cost, he chose not to receive Jesus as Lord. I'm praying he will yet change his mind and be open to make Jesus Lord of his life. But the seed is planted.

As I thought of my own journey and how I have changed, I suddenly realized how my eyes had opened to righteousness, because I found myself fighting the same fight as Jesus. This fight is encouraging people, at the risk of rejection and persecution, to open their eyes to God's truth and everlasting life, and to divert them from the road that results in judgement leading to spiritual death.

Spiritual Growth

When someone becomes a new believer, there is usually rapid spiritual growth as their eyes are opened to the truth. There are two scriptures I would like to highlight here about physical and spiritual growth. One is about John the Baptist, and the other about Jesus.

John the Baptist's father prophesied about the coming of Christ and how his son John would prepare the way for Him (Luke 1:67-79), and the words are so beautiful. Luke then tells us that John the Baptist grew and became strong in his spirit.

And the child grew and became strong in spirit; and he lived in the desert until he appeared publicly to Israel. (Luke 1:8)

Luke tells us that Jesus became not only strong physically, but also strong spiritually. He was filled with wisdom, and the grace of God was upon Him, which is a wonderful spiritual attribute. That is how it is with us. When the seed of God falls on fertile ground in our spirit, we will experience an amazing life changing growth.

> *'And the child grew and became strong; he was filled with wisdom, and the grace of God was upon him' (Luke 2:40).*

After salvation, Beryl and I grew enormously. My son mentioned to others that he has never seen someone change as radically as I did. To hear that from my son was hugely encouraging. For that growth to take place, however, I knew there was still a whole lot of changing needed in my life.

I needed help. I needed deliverance from previous wrong choices. Even though I had been a pastor for twelve years, it was only when we went for training at Ellel Ministries in the UK that we received the deeper ministry and counsel needed to break the bondages of the enemy over our lives.

Our lives took a 180-degree turn. Although we are eternally grateful for our church, it made us realize that there was a shortfall, not in the discipleship curriculum but in how to set people free. When we personally experienced real freedom, we realized what had been lacking in the discipleship program of our church.

It is common practice in local churches that, when people come for help, we don't know how to help them, and so we often refer them to secularly trained people without discerning or recognizing that they actually need spiritual help. Only the Church of Jesus Christ, properly trained in spiritual matters and with the help of the Holy Spirit, can set people free as Jesus did.

Secular counsellors may prescribe medication and help people to cope or live with their symptoms. However, true lasting healing requires that the root spiritual issues be identified and dealt with. I believe that such healing should be a normal part of church life and come though Christians operating under the anointing of the Holy Spirit.

Spirit Soul and Body

Of course, I'm not against any secular counselling. I do, from time to time, refer someone to a psychologist for assessment and ongoing therapy when it's not a spiritual issue. However, we need to recognize that, according to Scripture, there are three main areas in which we can be sick: the spirit, the soul and the body.

> *May God himself, the God of peace, sanctify you through and through. May your whole spirit, soul and body be kept blameless at the coming of our Lord Jesus Christ. (1 Thessalonians 5:23)*

The Body
In brief, when our body needs attention, we would generally go to a doctor or hospital for medical treatment.

The Soul
The soul comprises the mind, the will and our emotions. There are many reasons why we may need help in this area of our being. The way we think, the way we make decisions and the way we react in present situations reflect something of what has happened in the past. We frequently see great healing in individual's lives as they bring these issues before

Jesus with a willingness to forgive those who have hurt them, repent of any ungodly behavior of their own and have a desire to receive Jesus' healing and comfort.

In some cases, help from a psychologist or a psychiatrist may be helpful, and they may prescribe some form of medication to help the person. Ultimately, however, they can only help to control symptoms or help someone to cope with life, especially if the root issues are spiritual in nature.

The Spirit

I am referring here to the human spirit which is the core part of our being and includes our God-given identity and self-awareness. Paul writes that all three areas of who we are can be damaged, that is our spirit, soul and body. It should be noted that when one part is damaged the other parts of our being are often affected.

The secular, medical professionals may deal with the body and soul, but who can deal with the spirit of man except the Holy Spirit of God? Our spirit will live forever. We communicate with God, human spirit to God's Spirit. We worship Him in spirit and truth (John 4:24). How does the secular doctor or psychologist or psychiatrist deal with the human spirit? What medication can heal the human spirit?

Our human spirit can receive damage through constant abuse or shock and trauma. If we neglect healing to the human spirit, in time we may reach the point of just coping with life, but we will still carry damage and not be fully healed. Only God can heal our human spirit. We can easily understand that our body and soul can be damaged, but the fact that Paul includes our human spirit together with our soul and body implies that our spirit can be damaged and in need of healing.

The need to minister healing to the human spirit is not always understood, even by prayer ministry teams within the Church.

> *A happy heart makes the face cheerful, but heartache crushes the spirit. (Proverbs 15:13)*

> *The Lord is close to the brokenhearted and saves those who are crushed in spirit. (Psalm 34:18)*

Our own personal experience and the experience of praying with many, many Christians is that healing of the human spirit can be a vital step in the healing process. Erroneously and sadly, there are many within the greater Church Body that don't believe that the human spirit needs healing after salvation.

Christel's Testimony

Here is a testimony from Christel, who discovered for herself the reality of healing and deliverance:

'I grew up in a Christian home and in a church, which preached the Gospel clearly. As a result, I asked Jesus to come into my heart when I was only six years old. I grew up and remained in the same denomination for thirty-eight years and was privileged to be discipled in the basics of God's Word there. After my husband, Gary, and I got married, we served the Lord together, but we got to a place where we both felt 'stuck' and stagnant in our walk with the Lord.

On a camp we attended when our children were still quite young, we first encountered some teaching on healing and deliverance and realized that we had not been taught the full counsel of God. After waiting on God's direction for us, in 2001, He planted us in a church where we experienced the fullness of the Holy Spirit in a way we never had before. Yet we knew there was still more.

Our church had a heart for the broken, and after reading the book, 'Healing through Deliverance', by Peter Horrobin, and feeling a huge "Yes!" in my spirit regarding the truth I was reading in the pages of that book, I attended the 20-Day school at Shere House, Pretoria in 2008. The teaching, and subsequent healing and equipping journey that followed, enriched and deepened my relationship with the Lord, and brought understanding regarding aspects of God's Word that I have always just read without revelation of the truth it carried.

I had been a Christian for thirty-eight years, served the Lord faithfully, had a measure of God's truth, and yet lacked knowledge in fundamental and key areas of my Christian walk. Hebrews 6:1 says, *'Therefore let us move beyond the elementary teachings about Christ and be taken forward to maturity, not laying again the foundation of repentance from acts that lead to death, and of faith in God'*. I had been well taught in the *'elementary'* but lacked the *'solid food'* that Hebrews 5:14 speaks about.

I am so grateful that the Lord sees our hearts and always responds to those who hunger and thirst after righteousness. I am also grateful for my church as they embraced and encouraged my affiliation with Ellel

Ministries and then decided to partner with Ellel Ministries to help equip leaders and provide a safe place for healing.

Ellel Ministries has been invaluable to Gary and me, and we are now pastoring the very church where God planted us years ago. The team of Ellel Ministries has become part of our extended church family and a huge support to us personally and in our ministry. To God be the glory!'

In this chapter we have been looking at how our lives should be different when our eyes are opened, and we come out of the darkness. In the next chapter we will explore the need to be cleansed and healed of the consequences of living in the darkness.

Chapter 6
Cleansed from Darkness

Shortly after I got saved, I spent a lot of my time listening to good Bible teachers who were recommended to me by my pastor. However, I came across a teaching given to me by a friend. Those days we had cassette tapes. His teaching sounded good, a real evangelist, but there was something missing. He was explaining his heart for evangelism, getting people saved and motivating them to get out there and do the same. That was all well and good. In my own ignorance and enthusiasm, I went out thinking I could save the world.

In the first month after my salvation, I prayed for two men on their death beds in ICU wards. Both died. That did not deter me, and I went on to lead at least six people to the Lord in that first month. I was walking with my head in the clouds with excitement.

I could not really grasp the fact that Jesus had chosen me at the age of forty. Me? He died for my sins, He forgave me, and He knew me by name. It was incredible, and I just wanted to serve my new King. As time progressed, however, as excited as I was, I realized I was still doing the same ungodly things I had done before salvation.

I then heard a little about spiritual warfare and how Jesus had completely defeated Satan at the cross. I was told that all that was necessary to be set free was to remind the enemy of this fact. (Nothing was said about the need to deal with past hurt and pain in my life and to sincerely repent of my ungodly responses.)

So, I went to war in earnest, telling Satan that Jesus had set
me free, but nothing changed. At every altar call I was there
for a prayer to deliver me from this bondage or that evil spirit,
but it had little effect on my life. As much as I tried in my
own strength, I could not get to a place of living in victory.
All the prayer I received did not seem to help me to change.
I finally became resigned to the fact that the Christian life
consisted of constant warfare in the spirit with more defeats
than gains, and I assumed that everybody was in the same
position as me.

Cleansing and Freedom

I know that when Jesus went to the cross in our place, He
provided a way for our salvation. It is true that, when we use
our free will to repent of our sins and accept Jesus as our
Savior, we become a new creation, because we are made
alive in our human spirit as a result of Jesus coming into our
hearts and mixing with our spirit. Positionally our
relationship with God is made new. We are now reconciled
with God. We no longer have to be controlled by our old way
of life, and a new way of life can begin.

> *Therefore, if anyone is in Christ, he is a new
> creation; the old has gone, the new has come!
> (2 Corinthians 5:17)*

Through loving discipleship, we are now able to go through
the process of dealing with the consequences of our own sin
and the sins of others against us. We can bring our hurt, pain,
broken heartedness, and grief from the past to Jesus and
receive His comfort and healing. All the legal rights that we
gave to the enemy in our lives can now be dealt with. We can
receive cleansing and freedom from all the bondages that

Satan has put on our life. We can appropriate all that Jesus did for us on the cross and begin to experience the abundant life that Jesus promised.

But some Christians have been taught that everything from the past was dealt with the moment they made a decision for Jesus. This belief, that everything has been done at the cross, leaves the new believer thinking they are free when actually they are not. I have found that this teaching hinders new Christians from being open to receive all the healing and cleansing that Jesus wants to bring them, a process that has often been described as 'sanctification'.

God Wants to See us Healed

I stand amazed today that God used myself and Beryl to establish Telefriend and that I received a call into full time ministry in an amazing church. All I can think is that God saw my heart, the pain I suffered when I disappointed Him and my great desire to be free.

After twelve years in the pastorate, I believe God led us to meet Peter and Fiona Horrobin who founded Ellel Ministries in the UK. They told us a little of their healing and deliverance ministry, and my heart jumped for joy. It was three long years before we resigned as pastors and, at the age of fifty-eight, went to Ellel Ministries in England for further training.

After a couple of months of receiving amazing truths about living a Christian life of discipleship, and after getting healed from the effects of past abuse and sin in my life, joy and fear rose up in me at the same time. The truth of what Jesus did for me at the cross became a reality. Jesus died for my sins and I was forgiven. This is so important for every Christian to grasp, especially those struggling with the onslaught from the enemy.

The time came when I realized that these people at Ellel Ministries were safe, caring people who know how to deal with situations like mine. I decided to surrender myself, open up my soul and let them in, holding nothing back. Looking back on it now, I realize that, when we come to God for help, the 'dark night of the soul' does not last forever. It was tough, but I worked through my issues, and God gave me the breakthrough in the most incredible way. I thank God for loving, caring people at Ellel Ministries who knew how to deal with the brokenness in my life. The healing process was also a learning process.

When I was born again, I understood that Jesus had died on the cross for my sins and that I was a new creation washed by His blood. The biggest thing I learnt, as I received healing, was that discipling was also necessary to find healing for my past wounds.

These wounds were not only the consequence of what others had done to me, but also self-inflicted damage as a result of my own sins. I learnt that the enemy still had a hold on me because of the free will choices I had made in the past, thereby giving him a foothold or place in my life.

> *'In your anger do not sin: Do not let the sun go down while you are still angry, and do not give the devil a foothold.' (Ephesians 4:26-27)*

The Healing Ministry of Jesus

In Isaiah 61 the purpose of the coming Messiah is explained.

The Spirit of the Sovereign LORD is on me, because the LORD has anointed me to preach good news to the poor. He has sent me to bind up the brokenhearted, to proclaim freedom for the captives and release from darkness for the prisoners to proclaim the year of the LORD'S favor and the day of vengeance of our God, to comfort all who mourn. (Isaiah 61:1-2)

I am so grateful for the prayer ministry and deliverance I received and the freedom it brought into my life. What saddens me is that I believe there are many, many believers who, like me, have struggled for years after becoming Christians but have failed to experience the abundant life that Jesus promised. Their eyes have been closed to the healing and freedom from bondage that Jesus would want them to enjoy.

The problem is that many pastors and leaders don't know enough about the healing ministry of Jesus. The reason is that their senior leaders, up to the highest level in their denomination, have blocked any teaching about it, as they themselves have no understanding of Satan and his demonic kingdom. One could say they do not have a biblically based theology of good and evil, and so they decide to ignore or keep away from this vital area of Christian ministry. Some are just too fearful to venture into the basic biblical principle of setting captives free.

The problem is further aggravated because many theological seminaries, colleges and universities often don't teach on this subject. Their focus is generally on the eternal salvation we can receive as a result of Jesus going to the cross in our place.

Now, I'm not challenging the theology of that at all, but the hugely important aspect of how we can appropriate the victory of Jesus over Satan at the cross to bring healing, deliverance and freedom from bondage is often missing. If Jesus spent so much time teaching His disciples this hugely important aspect of ministry, why do so many churches ignore His teaching today?

Of course, I have no problem with teaching that Jesus died for our sins, paving the way for us to approach the throne of grace, and, in Jesus' name, we can confess our sins, repent and turn away from our sins. I have no problem with telling people to ask for forgiveness, forgive those who have sinned against us and open our hearts to receive Jesus as Lord of our lives.

> *... for all have sinned and fall short of the glory of God, (Romans 3:23)*

However, I do have a problem with some pastors teaching people that Jesus did it all for us at the cross, and there is nothing more to be done in our lives, using their interpretation of 2 Corinthians 5:17 to justify this position.

So, we see this tragic occurrence taking place: We, the Church, search for the lost - those with eyes spiritually closed - and we open their eyes to Jesus. However, if we do not teach and apply the full Gospel, we effectively close their eyes to the full healing Jesus provides. It's a case of eyes closed, eyes opened, and then eyes closed, or partially closed, to God's truth.

Are Church Members being Deprived?

I have observed that much preaching is about the 'kingdom of the church' rather than the Kingdom of God. Yet a primary focus of the ministry of Jesus was healing people of disease, sicknesses and driving out demon spirits. Peter, when speaking to the household of Cornelius, succinctly summarizes Jesus' ministry as follows:

> *You know how God anointed Jesus of Nazareth with the Holy Spirit and power, and how he went around doing good and healing all who were under the power of the devil, because God was with him. (Acts 10:38)*

I believe that church leaders, who do not practice the healing ministry of Jesus in its entirety, are depriving their members of their full inheritance of healing in Christ Jesus. This causes a major problem, because what is often proclaimed from the pulpit is at best only partial truth.

For instance, I have often heard it said in sermons that *"the truth will set you free."* Well yes, the truth will set you free, but firstly you have to *'know'* what that truth is. Secondly, there is a condition to knowing the truth and being set free. Let's look fully at the Scripture verses from which these quotes come. It's also always good to read the entire chapter making sure you have the verse in question in its context.

> *Jesus replied, To the Jews who had believed him, Jesus said, "If you hold to my teaching, you are really my disciples. Then you will know the truth, and the truth will set you free." (John 8:31-32)*

Yes, the truth will set you free, but preachers and teachers often fail to emphasize that freedom only comes when you 'know' the truth and that this 'knowing of the truth' only comes about when you meet the condition of holding on to Jesus' teaching. In other words, freedom comes about because we choose to live a life in obedience to the teaching of Christ.

Knowledge does not set you spiritually free. It's putting into practice in your heart that which you know to be truth which sets you free. Then, and only then, can you be set free. If you don't tell people that they need to put their life in order and hold onto the teachings of Jesus, they may find themselves in the position of a slave with no permanent place in God's family.

> *Jesus replied, "I tell you the truth, everyone who sins is a slave to sin. Now a slave has no permanent place in the family, but a son belongs to it forever. (John 8:34-35)*

> *For the time will come when men will not put up with sound doctrine. Instead, to suit their own desires, they will gather around them a great number of teachers to say what their itching ears want to hear. They will turn their ears away from the truth and turn aside to myths. (2 Timothy 4:3-4)*

The strategy of Satan, the prince of this world, is very cunning. He and his followers, called demons, which are fallen angels, use men and women to twist God's truth with persuasive and fine-sounding arguments. Worldly thinking today is mostly centered on self. Its focus is self-gain, greed, power and control. It is sad how this spirit has crept into the

Church. Paul, in his letter to Timothy, has strong words to say about how the enemy of our soul uses unhealed people in the Church to teach their own doctrine and not the full Gospel of Jesus.

> *If anyone teaches false doctrines and does not agree to the sound instruction of our Lord Jesus Christ and to godly teaching he is conceited and understands nothing. He has an unhealthy interest in controversies and quarrels about words that result in envy, strife, malicious talk, evil suspicions and constant friction between men of corrupt mind, who have been robbed of the truth and who think that godliness is a means to financial gain. But godliness with contentment is great gain. For we brought nothing into the world, and we can take nothing out of it. But if we have food and clothing, we will be content with that. People who want to get rich fall into temptation and a trap and into many foolish and harmful desires that plunge men into ruin and destruction. For the love of money is a root of all kinds of evil. Some people, eager for money, have wandered from the faith and pierced themselves with many griefs. (1 Timothy 6:3-10)*

Jesus is the Truth

To counter the deception and false doctrines, we need to know the truth. Jesus is the truth, but do we really know Jesus as we should? When we walk in His footsteps, day by day, night by night, not only at church on Sundays but at home, at work, at school or university, and even when alone behind closed doors, knowing the truth is so liberating. In John

So, Christians cannot be possessed by a demon, because they now belong to Jesus. But they can still have, or be oppressed by, a demon. Once the rights of the enemy have been removed, demons can be commanded to leave in the name of Jesus. The rights of the enemy are removed through confession of our own sins or forgiveness of others who have sinned against us. As we bring our lives into godly order, the enemy can be told to go.

> *Submit yourselves, then, to God. Resist the devil, and he will flee from you. (James 4:7)*

There may be other issues in a person's life which may need to be dealt with. For instance, wounding in the soul should not be mistaken for the need for deliverance. That is a separate issue. This is Holy Spirit ministry and, as Christian prayer ministers, we need to learn to be discerning of His leading. Stay clear of ministries using 'techniques'.

Let us look briefly at the ministry of deliverance which took place in the epistles. It happened after the cross and after Jesus had returned to Heaven. The early Christians continued in the footsteps of Jesus regarding ministry that involved the demonic. With the wise words of two of my colleagues, I would like to point out that "the Epistles are written mostly to help believers to avoid the need for deliverance (2 Corinthians 2:11), rather than how to do it. The book of Acts, however, records the action that was needed to help those who had been affected by the demonic realm."

> *Philip went down to a city in Samaria and proclaimed the Christ there. When the crowds heard Philip and saw the miraculous signs he did, they all paid close attention to what he said. With shrieks,*

evil spirits came out of many, and many paralytics and cripples were healed. So there was great joy in that city. (Acts 8:5-8)

How wonderful it would be to have all our churches active and witnessing the power of God! What joy that would bring! I can think of no better way of growing the Church. That was the disciples' model for growing Church (Acts 5:12-16). It will be even more so for us when we have the vision and the courage to take the ministry of Jesus into the marketplace.

Once when we were going to the place of prayer, we were met by a slave girl who had a spirit by which she predicted the future. She earned a great deal of money for her owners by fortune-telling. This girl followed Paul and the rest of us, shouting, "These men are servants of the Most High God, who are telling you the way to be saved." She kept this up for many days. Finally Paul became so troubled that he turned around and said to the spirit, "In the name of Jesus Christ I command you to come out of her!" At that moment the spirit left her. (Acts 16:16-18)

Now that really was marketplace ministry!

And God was doing extraordinary miracles by the hands of Paul, so that even handkerchiefs or aprons that had touched his skin were carried away to the sick, and their diseases left them and the evil spirits came out of them. (Acts 19:11-12 ESV)

Lynda's Testimony

Beryl and I first met Lynda, an Australian, at an Ellel Ministries conference in the UK, where Lynda shared her amazing testimony of healing. Here is her story in brief:

'I came to faith in Jesus Christ when I was twelve years old. At that time I simply wanted Jesus to be my 'special friend,' so I asked Jesus to come and live in my heart. He accepted the invitation! I then begun the greatest adventure of a lifetime - coming to know Jesus and to walk every day of my life with Him. In those early years there was so much I did not understand. My eyes were shut.

I grew up in a conservative evangelical church, which was good, but they, like many churches, were closed to many things that are clearly in the Bible. The healing and deliverance ministry of Jesus was one of those areas. Through a most extraordinary set of events Jesus opened my eyes to the truth and showed me that He indeed heals and delivers people today.

After school I originally studied to become a nurse and worked in a large city hospital. But I was restless. I wanted to learn more about Jesus and serve Him fully. So I left my full-time work and started studying with a small group of other like-minded young people doing a Missions Training School. It's not that I thought I was called to be a missionary. But I had a deep hunger to learn more about Jesus. I was happy to do whatever it was He wanted me to do.

As a part of the Missions Training School, the leaders set us physical challenges. These were to encourage us to trust Jesus in everything. One of these challenges was for our group to hike along an isolated ravine and camp in bush huts. We hiked along the deserted river all day. In an unexpected turn of events, the leaders forced us to hike back to our starting point in the dark rather than camping overnight.

I was really scared. I was not a hiker and to hike in the dark in the wild terrain was terrifying to me. I quickly fell to the back of the group, struggling with the demands of the hike. Walking in and out of the river, slipping on stones, hanging on to trees for balance, I was desperately trying to keep up. My torch was taken and given to another, so most of the time I was walking in near darkness.

At about 10.30 pm, when we were only a short walk from our destination, my foot slipped, and I started to fall. I thought I was going to fall into the river. I blacked out. I regained consciousness a few minutes later, feeling like I was in a nightmare. I had fallen 35 feet and landed amongst some rocks near the river.

Throughout the trauma of that night, as I waited for the paramedics to rescue me, I knew Jesus was with me. I was airlifted to hospital the next morning. My injuries included spinal and facial fractures and a mild brain injury. I was bruised all over to the point I was unrecognizable to my family.

How I had lived was nothing short of a miracle. But in the weeks and months that followed there was a brokenness inside me. It was tangible, like a broken mirror. I went through a very difficult time, living with constant pain and vertigo. This led to depression, to the point that I was suicidal, in a desperate cry to be free of the unrelenting pain. Even in those dark days, when I could not see or hear Him, Jesus was still with me.

Two and a half years after the accident Jesus led me to a conference. It was hosted by a group I had been involved with when I was nursing, called 'Health Care in Christ'. They had invited Ellel Ministries International directors, Peter and Fiona Horrobin, from England, to speak at the conference on evangelism, healing and deliverance.

Peter's teaching was gripping. I started to understand for the first time that Jesus could actually heal people today, and that people really could have demons that they could be set free from. My eyes were opened. Peter also taught on how Jesus can heal victims of accident and trauma. This was mind blowing!

Peter and Fiona offered to pray for me in front of the conference, and for the next few hours we all witnessed the unfolding of a miracle. As they prayed with me, I had to face a most difficult challenge. Peter said, "Lynda, can you forgive the leaders who forced you to go on that hike?" I knew that forgiving meant letting it go, no more complaining, and releasing them from all the disappointment, betrayal and anger I had felt. I knew if I didn't forgive, I would not be healed that night. I chose to forgive. I saw the face of Jesus before me smiling at me.

As the ministry continued, Jesus took me step by step through everything He knew I needed to be healed and set free. This included me receiving deliverance from demons, which I never knew I had until they were gone. By the end of the ministry, the physical pain had gone. As I faced the conference, full of beaming faces, I could feel that the inner brokenness was also gone. Jesus had made me whole.'

The full account of Lynda's story, including her battle to have her lifelong disability pension removed so she could work again, and how she went on to have a family, despite the prognosis that she would never be able to have children, can be found in the book, 'Lynda: From Accident & Trauma to Healing & Wholeness', by Lynda Scott (published by Sovereign World).

Learning the Lessons

When Jesus died on the cross, He fully paid the penalty for the sins of mankind. The consequences of sin, however, are dealt with after salvation, during the discipleship or sanctification process. The consequences of sin did not leave me when I received Jesus. Healing and deliverance are for today. I struggled through years of spiritual warfare, thinking I should be free, due to the many prayers I had received. I realized that the dear folk who prayed for me, well-meaning as they were, could only offer superficial prayers, because they were never dealing with the real issues of the consequences.

This is exactly why many people in the Body of Christ are not free. They were taught that everything is made new at salvation, and, as they are new creatures in Christ, they no longer need any sort of healing. This is false teaching and not borne out in reality.

If it were true, how do we explain why many Christians remain hooked on pornography, have extra marital affairs, get divorced, remain alcoholics or behave in other ungodly ways, just as they did before their salvation? But because they were taught that they didn't need healing after salvation, some Christians feel that they have to keep quiet and lie about their struggles. Some only finally get free of their inner conflict and sense of being a second-rate Christian, when they find a safe place, where there is an understanding of the need for healing.

We all need to learn how the reality of our life has affected us spiritually and shaped our perspective of God's truth. It might take some time, as it did for me, with wise people on the ministry team helping me. Now I can say, "Praise God! I am healed and delivered, and free to serve the Lord."

False Teaching

I heard of a pastor who was preaching a good message until he said, "If you, as a Christian, are still sinning, and if you're still in bondage to drugs, or you're struggling after salvation to be free of a demonic force like sexual lust, then I doubt your salvation." That is definitely wrong teaching!

False teaching tells you that, once you have accepted Jesus, you are now free from every hurt, disappointment, forgiveness issue, emotional and sexual soul ties, bondage, emotional pain and generational harassment. What these teachers are saying is that pain, condemnation and propensity to sin are no longer true for a Christian. But the truth is that if we have given the enemy of our soul legal rights through our wrong decisions, we now need to exercise our legal authority in Christ to cast him out.

This can only be done in the name of Jesus. In His name, the spirits still plaguing us in God's Kingdom must leave when we exercise our God-given authority. Then Satan and his demons no longer have rights over us, and we no longer belong to the father of lies. We now belong to Jesus, with God as our Father, the redeemer of our souls.

Only then, when Jesus sets us free, will we be free indeed, and not before. We are no longer in darkness but in the Kingdom of light - the Kingdom of God. When demons need to be dealt with, I strongly recommend you have an experienced Christian, who is well acquainted with deliverance, to minister to you.

> *This is the message we have heard from him and declare to you: God is light; in him there is no darkness at all. If we claim to have fellowship with him yet walk in the darkness, we lie and do not live by the truth. But if we walk in the light, as he is in the light, we have fellowship with one another, and the blood of Jesus, his Son, purifies us from all sin. If we claim to be without sin, we deceive ourselves and the truth is not in us. (1 John 1:5-8)*

The Lordship of Jesus

We need to consider whether we have made Jesus Lord over every area of our lives. For instance, we could have made Him Lord over our family but not over our finance, or Lord over our plans but not our sexuality. It is like the story Jesus taught about the woman mixing dough. It only needs a little bit of yeast to affect the whole of the dough.

I like to use the analogy of an orange. An orange has different segments. Imagine each segment has a name concerning aspects of my life, such as, my attitudes, my beliefs, my work, my marriage, my sexuality, my body, my looks, and my exercise habits. I may have given the Lord control over one area but not another. Therefore, ask yourself this question: "Is Jesus Lord over every area of my life?"

The parts of my life where He is not Lord are the areas where Satan will still have a hold on me. Those parts need to be submitted to Him. When we come under Jesus' covering or protection, we want the whole of us to be under His umbrella, not just part of us.

You can do this by praying in the following way:

"Jesus, I give you the broken parts in this area (name it) of my life. I confess my sin in this area and I am sorry and ask You to forgive me. I ask, Lord, that You begin a healing in this area and help me not to return to my old ways. Please help me to resist any temptation that comes my way. Thank You, Lord Jesus."

Without repentance and asking God for forgiveness, why would Jesus set you free? He knows you would go right back into sin because your heart is not right. Suppose you are a Christian who is living in sin. It would not be helpful for you to ask someone to pray for you to set you free from an evil spirit, without first repenting of your sins. God requires sin to be confessed and spoken out. So, find a 'safe' person who knows how to respect your confidentiality and who can pray for you. This scripture will help you understand what I'm trying to convey to you.

> *'Therefore confess your sins to each other and pray*
> *for each other so that you may be healed. The prayer*
> *of a righteous man is powerful and effective' (James*
> *5:16).*

Whoever would want to continue living in darkness, or even half-darkness, which is sometimes called the twilight zone? Confess those inner dark places and be healed and set free.

> *The one who calls you is faithful and he will do it.*
> *(1 Thessalonians 5:24)*

There may be a deep, painful area of your life, perhaps abuse from a loved one, that you've pushed down and hidden in your 'emotional basement'. It's a dark area in your life. It was not your fault, but you are concerned about what others would say if it ever came out into the open.

Some people are hurt and have deep emotional pain which is an area that is sensitive and raw inside them. They need individual attention to deal with and work through old wounds which have never healed. Personal caring and loving attention is required. A confidential person or ministry like Ellel Ministries could help to set you free.

When we are willing to repent of our sinful behavior and attitudes and are willing to choose to forgive those who have sinned against us, we can appropriate into our lives all that Jesus won for us at Calvary. We can take away the rights given to Satan, tell him to leave and enter more fully into the abundant life that Jesus came to bring.

In the next chapter we will look at the problem of wrong use or misinterpretation of scriptures, and hence false teaching, that cause our eyes to be closed to the wonderful truths of God's word.

Chapter 7
False Teaching

Through our involvement in Telefriend and Ellel Ministries, Beryl and I come into contact with Christians from many different backgrounds and traditions. We have been privileged to meet and pray with many pastors and leaders. We hear many wonderful stories of what God is doing in the lives of individuals and in the church they attend. But we also hear many heart-breaking stories of struggles and challenges as a result of the undermining of leaders, spiritual abuse by leaders, church splits and the consequences of false teaching and doctrinal practices.

In this chapter I want to look at the subject of false teaching and false teachers within the Church. My prayer is that my words will not come across purely as criticism but rather that your spiritual eyes will be opened to the reality of what can happen. Furthermore, my prayer is that the Holy Spirit will show you if you are holding on to beliefs or doctrinal practices that are not fully in accord with God's truth.

What makes a False Teacher

Jesus warns us to always be on the lookout for false teachers and prophets. But what makes a 'false' teacher? I believe it is someone who teaches their own form of religion or misquotes the Bible, totally distorting its meaning. How about those who only choose what they want to believe, so they teach some truth and ignore what they don't want to believe? Either way, where the full truth is not proclaimed, it constitutes false teaching.

With our spiritual eyes open, we should believe every truth revealed to us in the Bible. The New Testament is a record of the era in history where Jesus came to teach us who Father God really is and to lead us to the right path for entering the Kingdom of God.

Before returning to His Father in heaven, Jesus commissioned us, His disciples (collectively referred to as the Church), to continue His work on Earth. If we are to do this, it is vitally important that we read and learn the Scriptures and follow His instructions. It is not only a matter of knowing Scripture, but of also doing the work that Jesus did.

Every part of Jesus' public ministry was recorded by those who were close to Him. He taught what we call the 'hear, see, and do method'. He taught them, He showed them how, and then He sent them out to do the same. In the two thousand years which have passed since Jesus came, this has never changed.

The fact that much of His Church no longer practices what He taught does not mean that what He taught is not for today, that it is old fashioned, or that everything has already been dealt with at the cross. We are warned not to leave anything out of the Scriptures and not to add anything to them. The Word of God does not lie and is complete truth. If Jesus taught His disciples how to heal the sick and set captives free, this ministry must still be for today. Don't let anyone persuade you otherwise and close your eyes to this vital truth.

Every word of God is flawless; he is a shield to those who take refuge in him. Do not add to his words, or he will rebuke you and prove you a liar. (Proverbs 30:5-6)

These are strong words, and they still apply to today. Anyone trying to refute this scripture, and many others in a similar vein, are in danger of falling into the 'false teacher' category. We should not solely rely on the teachers and preachers to expound the truth to us. However amazing they may be, and whatever educational certificates they may have, we have a responsibility to confirm what is biblical and what is not. Every one of us is able to receive revelation from God's word by the Holy Spirit.

But when he, the Spirit of truth, comes, he will guide you into all truth. He will not speak on his own; he will speak only what he hears, and he will tell you what is yet to come. He will bring glory to me by taking from what is mine and making it known to you. All that belongs to the Father is mine. That is why I said the Spirit will take from what is mine and make it known to you. (John 16:13-15)

We may be relying on teachers of the Bible to be honest and give us the whole truth, but I'm sad to say, this is not always so. However anointed and persuasive they may seem to be, we need to have discernment about what they are teaching. We also need to be aware of what they are leaving out and not teaching from the Bible.

They may be spiritually starving us by not giving us the full Gospel. It is the Church's responsibility to continue to teach the original doctrine handed down from the apostles in Scripture. There is much which threatens to rob us of faith and biblical beliefs. For instance, if we are not being taught about being filled or baptized in the Holy Spirit and the spiritual gifts, are we being *'guided into all truth?'* What spiritual riches there are in the Bible! God has so much for His Church. How tragic that so much of it has been ignored!

> *I pray that out of his glorious riches he may strengthen you with power through his Spirit in your inner being, so that Christ may dwell in your hearts through faith. And I pray that you, being rooted and established in love, may have power, together with all the saints, to grasp how wide and long and high and deep is the love of Christ, and to know this love that surpasses knowledge—that you may be filled to the measure of all the fullness of God. Now to him who is able to do immeasurably more than all we ask or imagine, according to his power that is at work within us, to him be glory in the church and in Christ Jesus throughout all generations, for ever and ever! Amen. (Ephesians 3:16-21)*

Our heritage and equipping as children of God gives us confidence about who we are in Christ Jesus. It is the foundation from which we develop our personal ministry to serve our King of kings. So, we need to ask important questions. What am I being taught to believe? Is it man's way or God's way?

Hundreds of 'interpretations' of the Bible could so easily take us off track. Are there vital truths which are being ignored and which are keeping us in darkness? Ask the Lord to show you what is hidden from your sight and to shine His light into that darkness.

We need to be filled with the Holy Spirit so we can discern God's truth. We are then in a good position to choose to obey God. The apostle Peter and the other Christians were put in prison and commanded to stop preaching about Jesus. After they were miraculously set free from the prison, they continued to preach the Gospel, and when they were interrogated and accused by the authorities of being disobedient, they bravely answered that they had to obey God rather than men.

> *Peter and the other apostles replied: "We must obey God rather than men!" (Acts 5:29)*

Tradition or Truth

The truth is that many of our spiritual leaders are unable to teach God's biblical truth because they have been so influenced by years of church traditions. They have made compromises and failed to bring needful correction to those under their care. Some have even fallen into secret sin and become too ashamed to preach truth. Personal sin in anyone's life is wrong, but in a leader, it affects the whole church.

When Spirit-filled believers are not given any opportunity to do prayer ministry, healing will not be present in that church. Healing must include setting Christians free from demonic activity in their lives, otherwise the enemy will certainly cause them to be blown *'here and there by every wind of teaching and by the cunning and craftiness of men in their deceitful scheming'. (Ephesians 4:14)*

Let's take a look at biblical truths which are sometimes removed or replaced by church traditions. The Christian Church needs to be active and purposeful in evangelism, leading people into the necessity of being born again, and highlighting and practicing the teachings of Jesus about the Kingdom of God. Adult baptism rather than infant baptism should be offered, the instruction to believers to be filled with the Holy Spirit should be clearly taught, and the gifts of the Spirit should be encouraged. The church should offer healing for those who are sick and should be preaching and practicing the Gospel, which includes setting captives free.

> *On a Sabbath Jesus was teaching in one of the synagogues, and a woman was there who had been crippled by a spirit for eighteen years. She was bent over and could not straighten up at all. When Jesus saw her, he called her forward and said to her, "Woman, you are set free from your infirmity." Then he put his hands on her, and immediately she straightened up and praised God. (Luke 13:10)*

There is so much available for us in the Church as we put into practice what Jesus taught. We need to have the courage to obey God's word rather than human rules. Fourteen times in Scripture we read that Jesus cautioned His disciples to be on their guard against false teachers who will always be present amongst us. The words recorded in Mark 7 that Jesus spoke out to the Pharisees are very sobering.

> *"Isaiah was right when he prophesied about you hypocrites; as it is written: 'These people honor me with their lips, but their hearts are far from me. They worship me in vain; their teachings are merely human rules.' You have let go of the commands of God and are holding on to human traditions." And he continued, "You have a fine way of setting aside*

the commands of God in order to observe your own
traditions!" (Mark 7:6-9)

Ask the Lord to open your eyes to the Scriptures and allow
them to burn in your heart. After His resurrection, Jesus was
talking to two believers on the road to Emmaus, and, as they
walked along, He was teaching them; yet their eyes were still
closed even with Jesus right beside them. It wasn't until Jesus
broke the bread at the meal table and gave it to them that they
recognized who He was.

Then their eyes were opened and they recognized
him, and he disappeared from their sight. They
asked each other, "Were not our hearts burning
within us while he talked with us on the road and
opened the Scriptures to us?" (Luke 24:31-32)

How often do people attend a church service, week after
week, with their spiritual eyes closed? If someone comes
along and speaks truth to them, such as, "Jesus says we must
be born again", it sounds so strange to their ears that they find
it difficult to believe. They have never been taught that in the
church before.

It's good to listen to lovely, encouraging words from the
Bible week after week and year after year, but if people don't
get this vital teaching, does it mean the spiritual leaders are
unconcerned whether people have a personal relationship
with Jesus and can be assured of eternal life after death?
When Jesus walked along the Emmaus road, He was opening
the eyes of those two to truth. God's truth changes our lives
forever.

Equipped for Service

All Scripture is God-breathed and is useful for teaching, rebuking, correcting and training in righteousness, so that the man of God may be thoroughly equipped for every good work. (2 Timothy 3:16-17)

Are God's men and women being taught to '*be thoroughly equipped for every good work?*' If the fullness of the Word of God is not being taught, it removes the power and authority of God, which He freely gives to every born-again Christian to cast out demons, heal the sick, preach the Gospel and cure diseases. If we are not ministering in the power of God, as Jesus did, we are not in total obedience to His instruction to go into all the world.

There is a dark and sick world out there waiting for our obedience. Much of the time they wait in vain. Jesus' disciples were following Him from village to village, and they learnt by carefully watching Him. They heard, they saw and then He sent them out to do what He did. They were doing the work of God the Father.

But we ought always to thank God for you, brothers loved by the Lord, because from the beginning God chose you to be saved through the sanctifying work of the Spirit and through belief in the truth. (2 Thessalonians 2:13)

Paul encourages the Ephesians and prays for them to have the Spirit of wisdom and revelation so that they may know God the Father better. Jesus always points us to Father, and the more we know the Father, the less resistance we will have to do the work Jesus taught us to do.

> *I keep asking that the God of our Lord Jesus Christ, the glorious Father, may give you the Spirit of wisdom and revelation, so that you may know him better. I pray also that the eyes of your heart may be enlightened in order that you may know the hope to which he has called you, the riches of his glorious inheritance in the saints, and his incomparably great power for us who believe. That power is like the working of his mighty strength, which he exerted in Christ when he raised him from the dead and seated him at his right hand in the heavenly realms, far above all rule and authority, power and dominion, and every title that can be given, not only in the present age but also in the one to come. And God placed all things under his feet and appointed him to be head over everything for the church, which is his body, the fullness of him who fills everything in every way. (Ephesians 1:17-23)*

We need desperately to *'know the hope to which He has called us ... and his incomparably great power for us who believe'*.

We cannot afford to be ignorant of the scriptures that have a direct bearing on our life on Earth. We, His people, constitute the Church, and we need to live as Jesus intended us to. Some church traditions give the idea that it doesn't matter how we live during the week. On Sunday we can just ask for forgiveness again and get it sorted out. Contrast that with the way true Christian believers live. They choose to come together for worship on Sunday, or whatever day they choose, and they gladly give thanks for all God has done during the week. Without healing through the sanctifying work of the Holy Spirit, the Church will remain a weak Church without God's power and without a voice to the nations. Jesus asked the Pharisees a penetrating and challenging question in Matthew 15:3.

> *Jesus replied, "And why do you break the command of God for the sake of your tradition? (Matthew 15:3)*

I have a spiritually astute friend who keeps abreast with world affairs and the spiritual implications it has on the Church. He once said to me that he wondered whether the state of any nation was a reflection of the state of the Church in that nation. This really got me thinking, and it is something for us all to ponder on.

Denominational Christianity

Christians believe that Jesus Christ was born of the Virgin Mary, that He is the Son of God, that He died on the cross for our sins, that He descended into hell and on the third day He arose from the grave, that He was taken up bodily in the clouds to His Father in Heaven and now sits at the right hand of God the Father.

They believe that Jesus is God, and He will return the same way that He ascended into Heaven. These statements are mostly about *who* Jesus is and not *how* He discharged His ministry. I believe it is mainly about the topic of how Jesus carried out His ministry where differences come in that keep Christians apart, causing disunity and mistrust.

Denominational Christianity is extremely powerful. The Bible confirms that, when two or more come together in agreement, God will be with us. Typically, the devil will want to do his counterfeit of this. When two or more come together in ungodly agreement, he, the devil, will want to be part of that agreement to give it power.

Churches and denominations generally create doctrinal practices based on a consensus of their theological understanding. Baptism is a good example of this, whereby some say we should only baptize adults, whilst others say we should baptize babies. Should any of the leadership or members disagree with the stated doctrinal practice, there would be sharp dispute.

Even if the general belief was out of line with God's Word, it would be difficult for individual leaders or a whole denomination to change. It would take a miracle for a leader to be able to confess that they were wrong, repent, ask for forgiveness and change their practice.

There are many differences of opinion between church groups. Not all are wrong and not all are right. Much of what is discussed in this book would be a challenge for many. Some might choose to ignore what I believe God is saying to us, His Church, whilst others might be convicted to *'seek first the Kingdom of God and His Righteousness'* and pursue being the effective Church Jesus called us to be.

The influence of senior leaders over other leaders to protect their traditional spiritual beliefs will definitely come into play. Standing for truth may mean having to make a choice between leaving one's church or compromising God's Word.

It's tough. But in the end, God's blessing comes from standing for truth and obeying Him rather than human rules.

A Difficult Choice

When a church leader finds a major truth is not practiced in their denomination, what can they do? Either they can ignore biblical truth, or they need to speak out and risk being thrown out of their position. It's not an easy decision whether to follow one's denominational beliefs and stay, or follow one's convictions and leave? It should be a case of, "God, what do You want me to do?"

I have experienced what it's like to be in a church for many years and then have God ask me to make that choice. By choosing to leave, I felt as if I was betraying my spiritual family members. After discussing my dilemma with my leaders, and realizing the system was not going to change, I made the costly decision to follow God's way. Over the years, I've seen friends come to a similar crossroads, but they have chosen to stay, only to remain in a place of no spiritual growth.

I was asked to minister in a denominational church which believes in infant baptism. I have no problem with infant dedication, but I don't agree with calling it 'baptism' and using water, because baptism has to do with submerging. I believe that adults have to make their own decision to be baptized.

It was a course which ran over a number of days. One of the leaders in this church who was on the course asked if I would baptize him and his family. Now, here was my dilemma. I knew the church frowned on adult baptism, and some of their people didn't want to leave the church, but they did want to be baptized. Would I, in this instance, bow to the fear of man, or would I obey what I believe is scripturally right?

I finally agreed to baptize the family, knowing that this decision would be frowned upon. I was taken by surprise on the day appointed for the baptism. Not only did the family come for baptism, but as I finished baptizing the family, another person said that they also wanted to be baptized and entered the water fully clothed. Then another said they wanted to be baptized.

There was such an anointing of God's presence around that pool. Unexpectedly, seventeen more people, all from the same church, walked into that swimming pool fully clothed, wanting to be obedient to God's command to be baptized. God's presence was so tangible. As expected, I was in trouble with the church leaders, but I was not disobedient to God.

I love Kingdom ministry. Although I am a member of a local church, my ministry is more Kingdom based. My wife and I and our team have the privilege to minister in many different denominational churches as well as independent churches. We teach about the Kingdom of God, as opposed to the kingdom of the church. I thank God for leaders who have heard teachings about the Kingdom of God and have begun a journey in finding out how their church can be more effective. I rejoice that the power of God is returning to their churches.

Setting Captives Free

Let's look at a teaching that is in the Bible, which is undoubtedly touched upon by universities or seminaries, yet in many cases is not taught in such a way that it can be applied today to those who need release from spiritual bondage.

> *Jesus returned to Galilee in the power of the Spirit, and news about him spread through the whole countryside. He taught in their synagogues, and everyone praised him. He went to Nazareth, where he had been brought up, and on the Sabbath day he went into the synagogue, as was his custom. And he stood up to read. The scroll of the prophet Isaiah was handed to him. Unrolling it, he found the place where it is written: "The Spirit of the Lord is on me, because he has anointed me to preach good news to the poor. He has sent me to proclaim freedom for the prisoners and recovery of sight for the blind, to release the oppressed, to proclaim the year of the Lord's favor." Then he rolled up the scroll, gave it back to the attendant and sat down. The eyes of everyone in the synagogue were fastened on him, and he began by saying to them, "Today this scripture is fulfilled in your hearing." (Luke 4:14-21)*

Jesus chose to read a passage from the scroll of Isaiah which focused on setting the captives free, but I know of some churches that stay well clear of this passage and other scriptures to do with the healing and deliverance ministry. These churches may lead people into the way of salvation, but they stop short of helping their people to be free from past hurts or their dealings with the occult.

Other churches don't even bother to teach the Good News of salvation. My wife and I were in one of these churches. At the age of twenty-five we were married in this church, and the minister became a family friend. I even served on the church council for a while. How often I tried to read my Bible, but it made no sense to me! Unfortunately, we never heard the biblical truth of the need to be 'born again', that is until we moved to another town and visited another church at the age of forty. Everything in my life changed then.

As much as we loved going to that first church and meeting such tremendously faithful people, we have to say that they were ignorant of the truth of the Gospel. Each one, like me, was trapped in a denomination and its traditions.

I can now look back over many years of ministry, helping people to find salvation in Jesus, seeing others healed from their traumatic past, and setting people free from the consequences of the past, from fear, rejection, abuse and bondages. It's amazing to see the power of Jesus' name expel darkness from their lives as they humbly repent of ungodly activities that they have been involved in. All this has been done in the lives of Christians who have made a commitment to the Lord Jesus, some of them more than fifty years ago.

Three Challenging Questions

There are three big questions I ask myself again and again. I hope that these are questions no one would ever dare to ignore.

The first one is this: "If I, as a church leader, am not doing the work of Jesus here on earth, helping people to know Jesus and teaching them to set people free from the deception and power of the enemy, what excuse am I going to give to God on the day I come face to face with Him and have to give an account of my life?" Jesus warned us that it's all about our relationship with Him.

> *Not everyone who says to me, 'Lord, Lord,' will enter the kingdom of heaven, but only he who does the will of my Father who is in heaven. Many will say to me on that day, 'Lord, Lord, did we not prophesy in your name, and in your name drive out demons and perform many miracles?' Then I will tell them plainly, 'I never knew you. Away from me, you evildoers!' (Matthew 7:21)*

The second question is this: "If I don't forgive those who hurt me, abandoned me, rejected me, abused me, didn't teach me to be a true disciple of Jesus or deceived me by not telling me the truth, will my Father in Heaven forgive me for my sins?"

> *For if you forgive men when they sin against you, your heavenly Father will also forgive you. But if you do not forgive men their sins, your Father will not forgive your sins. (Matthew 6:14-15)*

The third question is this: "If I am not doing what Jesus did, am I a false teacher?"

> *"Watch out for false prophets. They come to you in sheep's clothing, but inwardly they are ferocious wolves. By their fruit you will recognize them. Do people pick grapes from thornbushes, or figs from thistles? Likewise every good tree bears good fruit, but a bad tree bears bad fruit. A good tree cannot bear bad fruit, and a bad tree cannot bear good fruit. Every tree that does not bear good fruit is cut*

*down and thrown into the fire. Thus, by their fruit
you will recognize them. " (Matthew 7:15-20)*

But for each one of us…

*But seek first his kingdom and his righteousness,
and all these things will be given to you as well.
(Matthew 6:33)*

It is never too late to turn from our ways, ask the Lord for His
forgiveness and earnestly serve the Lord our God in the
Name of Jesus Christ our Lord and Savior.

*Repent, then, and turn to God, so that your sins may
be wiped out, that times of refreshing may come
from the Lord. (Acts 3:19-20)*

In this chapter we have looked at how the traditions of man
can result in eyes becoming closed to Jesus' great
commission to His Church. In the next chapter we will
explore how Satan uses deception in both the world and the
Church to try and thwart the establishment of God's
Kingdom here on earth.

Chapter 8
Beware of Deception

Before we met Jesus as our personal Savior, Beryl and I already had compassion for the broken hearted. Whilst we were pioneering 'Life Line' in Windhoek, Namibia, in the late 1970's, an event took place that was the beginning of change in my life and that of my family.

Early one morning, around 03:00 am, while I was on all night telephone duty, I received a call from a lady who was in deep emotional stress. It was probably the worst, and yet the best, call I ever had. As I listened to her situation and was asking appropriate questions to get an accurate understanding of her mixed-up situation, I found I had nothing I could suggest or adequately console her with.

Although she seemed happy that she could speak to someone who was trying to understand, she knew that there was truly nothing anyone could do for her. There was something in that call that disturbed me deeply. I knew there was something missing, and there was a hollowness in my attempt to bring hope.

After my duty I went home that morning for a shower. While telling Beryl of my experience, I said to her, *"This is God's work, and we need to get closer to Him"*. That admission spoken out into the heavenlies was a defining moment in our lives. Had my eyes opened to a spiritual truth? Holding on to this inner excitement, I knew it was something I had to pursue.

I approached my minister and three other ministers of different denominations whom I knew vaguely. My request to them was for help to show me how to get closer to God. Each one encouraged me, saying, "Keep going. You're on the right track". But I found they were either too busy, or their circuit was too big, so they could not mentor me. Although I was not sure what I was asking them, I came away from each meeting sensing that the good work I was doing was the right way to God. It was like a hit-or-miss journey. Either you make it or you don't.

Missed Opportunity

Not one of them spoke to me about salvation and how the journey of getting close to the Lord was a personal walk. As I was relating my desire to get closer to God with the fourth pastor, and getting much the same response as before, I burst into tears in his office. I had no idea why I reacted that way, and I was rather embarrassed.

As I look back at that time, I felt the Lord saying that I was crying tears on His behalf, expressing His frustration about the earthly representatives of His Church. These pastors had missed their opportunity to shine like stars.

> *Those who are wise will shine like the brightness of the heavens, and those who lead many to righteousness, like the stars for ever and ever. (Daniel 12:3)*

It was as if the experience of that brief, spiritual awakening which had taken place after I had spoken to the lady on the phone in the dead of night was not real. It's as if my spiritual eyes, which the Holy Spirit had opened, had been closed again by the ministers of His Church. Today, this is a deep concern for me, as I know there are many in the Church who are seeking, but they are given the impression that if they keep on coming to church, they will be fine. But people's hearts are so ripe for a deeper relationship with the Father. I wonder if they are under a false impression of what salvation is. Have they, by their own free will, invited Jesus into their hearts?

Two years later, when I was forty, we moved to Pretoria due to a company transfer. We joined 'Life Line' in Pretoria and I soon became the chairman of the then Northern Transvaal Centre in Pretoria. Beryl became the secretary to the Centre leader. Through a set of circumstances and meeting new people in Pretoria, we were invited to a Hatfield Christian Church service, a local charismatic church.

Coming from a traditional mainline church, I had never been to, or even heard of, a charismatic church. It was so different from the traditional church we had known all our lives. As a young boy I was an altar worker and later, after we got married, I was a church deacon in another denomination.

Although we felt uncomfortable on that first visit to Hatfield, for the first time we heard the truth of the Gospel. It certainly threw me into a spin. Why had we never heard the truth of the Gospel before? We enjoyed what we heard and went back for more, every time with more questions than answers. One day, after attending a number of services, we had a visit from Ivan Vorster, one of the local Hatfield Christian Church pastors. He answered all my questions and then he popped the most important, caring question which I'd never heard before; "Would you like to receive Jesus Christ as your Lord and Savior?" From deep within, my answer was a spontaneous "Yes!"

Would I have gone to heaven had I died before this time? The simple answer is 'no'. But a bigger question is how those four pastors will answer to the Lord one day. These four pastors were on the top of my list of people to forgive.

A Sobering Thought

Reflecting on the years, long before I was married, gives me a cold shudder down my spine. After attending a German October Fest Carnival in Windhoek, Namibia, I had too much to drink and had a high-speed motorcar accident in the Aris Hills, south of Windhoek.

I now know that had I died in that accident I wouldn't have gone to heaven. Why not? Because although I went to church occasionally, I had never acknowledged Jesus Christ as my Savior by using my free will to invite Him into my heart to live in me and me in Him.

I never heard this minister friend of mine preach or speak about salvation. Did he deceive me, or was he himself in deception about the Word of God? I don't know, but many follow the words of good, respected men and women rather than the truth of the Word of God.

We thought that, as we were there in that church and believed in God and the principles of the Christian faith, we would automatically qualify for Heaven. Somehow the enemy had successfully closed our eyes to scriptures such as Romans 10:9-10.

That if you confess with your mouth, "Jesus is Lord," and believe in your heart that God raised him from the dead, you will be saved. For it is with your heart that you believe and are justified, and it is with your mouth that you confess and are saved. (Romans 10:9-10)

Beryl and I had been attending a traditional church on and off for nearly fifteen years before we even heard that we needed to be 'born again'. It was another nineteen years, including twelve years serving as a pastor, before we discovered that healing and freedom for the issues of life which were bugging me, were available through ministry. I don't think our experience was in any way unique, but it is a testimony to how successful Satan has been in subtly diverting the Church away from its primary mission to make 'effective' disciples.

Making Disciples

That word 'make', or 'create', leaves me with the feeling that something new has to come out of something that already exists. Making a disciple means helping a believer to become the person God intended them to be. This involves helping them to be free of worldly thinking and ungodly behavior.

The process can be likened to a potter taking a lump of clay and molding it into a useful vessel. First of all, the potter needs to remove impurities such as small stones, bits of old grass or twigs that, otherwise, will hamper the molding process and make the finished article unfit for its purpose.

It is best for a new believer, who comes out of the world and stops believing lies about who God is, to receive ministry as soon as possible. New disciples need encouraging and guidance in how they can make Jesus Lord of their life. Then we need to explain to them how past ungodly relationships or various bondages may be controlling their lives and how these and other impurities can be removed by the Master Potter.

These could include such things as lust for money or addiction to smoking, alcohol or pornography, and sex outside of marriage. They need to understand that they have a part to play. They need to choose to trust and allow God to start working in their lives. For them to be free from all the burdens and blockages preventing them from drawing closer to God, they may need to receive inner healing and even a measure of deliverance.

The idea that new Christians may need deliverance is not a new idea. In this regard it is interesting to read what Hippolytus (a teacher and presbyter in the church at Rome) wrote in about 236 AD:

> *'From the day they are chosen let a hand be laid on them and let them be exorcised daily. And when the day draws near on which they are to be baptized, let the bishop himself exorcise each one of them, that he may be certain that he is purified. But if there is one who is not purified let him be put on one side because he did not hear the word of instruction with faith. For the evil and strange spirit remained with him.' (Apostolic Traditions)*

Alrika's Testimony

I would like to stress the vital need for a person who has experienced any sort of trauma to seek prayer ministry to deal with the emotional tension which builds up inside. Some don't like the word 'inner healing', but actually, that's what it is. Many people live with emotional pain day in and day out. In Christ Jesus there is hope and freedom. Here is a testimony of one such person who received healing from a most horrific experience.

Alrika has kindly offered to share the story of her healing journey. She experienced severe loss and trauma when her husband and two young daughters were all killed in a motor accident.

'I was sitting on the floor of the bedroom in my parents' house, unpacking our broken laptop and the bag I took from the wreckage. Everything inside was broken and destroyed - just as my life, my family and my livelihood had been broken and destroyed with the car crash the previous day. My head and my feelings were numb with shock, and thinking about the road ahead, the only words I could muster were, "Father, I cannot do this. You will have to take me through this journey".

I had accepted Jesus as my Savior years before, and my relationship with the Lord was the center of my life. Yes, there had been tough and difficult times, when I was on a steep learning curve, but also excitement, joy and thankfulness. God loved me and used the wasted years of my life to His glory, as I steadily drew ever closer to Him.

As a family we were active members of our church and loved being part of the Body of Christ. I joined Telefriend early in my spiritual journey, drawn by a compassion for hurting people. I learned that we are only the vessels that God uses to bring truth to people, but that it is He who brings healing. The years of reading and studying God's Word were a saving grace after the accident.

Due to the shock and trauma I struggled to read, but His word was in my heart. When I spiraled downwards, His Word was the wind beneath my wings (albeit broken wings) that kept me from the depression that everyone expected me to fall into. I clung to His promises with all the strength I had left over.

Sitting in the 'ashes' of my life, the room with the bodies of my husband and two daughters, a verse from the Bible came to my mind: 'and provide for those who grieve in Zion— to bestow on them a crown of beauty instead of ashes, the oil of joy instead of mourning and a garment of praise instead of a spirit of despair' (Isaiah 61:3). That is what I believed, even though I could not fathom out what the journey ahead would be.

Somehow the healing I so desperately needed for my mind, my emotions, my physical body, and my broken human spirit was not to be found in a formal church setting. Although there was truth, spoken in love and certain hope, it just did not address the deep ache, the sleeplessness and sense of belonging which had been stolen.

After a few months I started attending courses at Ellel ministries. Initially I thought I would just do this to learn how to help others. Little did I know that God's heart for me was for me to be healed completely – and not just of the shock and trauma of the accident. He knew where I needed help.

With each biblical truth that was taught on the course God had me look at my own life and my own heart. Since early childhood I had made mistakes and done wrong things, as well as being hurt by others. But I had covered up those areas in my life with 'false' beliefs and ungodly actions.

I needed to acknowledge those sins and hurts and bring them to the Lord for forgiveness and healing. I was led through the various steps to healing; repentance, accepting God's forgiveness, forgiving others, acknowledging the lies I had believed and allowing them to be replaced by God's truths.

God brought inner healing and deliverance to the loss in my life. He healed me so much that I can truly say I am walking my journey of life with joy again, and in a freedom which I never knew before'.

Return to your rest, my soul, for the LORD has been good to you. For you, LORD, have delivered me from death, my eyes from tears, my feet from stumbling, that I may walk before the LORD in the land of the living. (Psalms 116:7-9)

'Not only did God restore my mind, emotions, and human spirit, but He placed me in another family again with a husband who cherishes me. As I sit on the veranda of our house, looking out over the wild bushland, my heart rejoices, and I am full of thankfulness. I can't humanly understand everything about my healing, but I know God has done it.'

It's a wonderful testimony of what God can do. Alrika is free of the emotional pain associated with the trauma. Her memories remain, but they no longer trigger into her emotions.

Worldly-Thinking Leaders

The enemy of our souls is hard at work bombarding Christian minds with lies about who God really is. These lies are pressurizing people to feel they are wrong in their biblical thinking, and it causes them to doubt their faith.

Unfortunately, worldly-thinking Christian Church leaders are not adding to the cause for God's Kingdom, and they are confusing their congregation members about what is truth by agreeing with those lies. Immature and undiscerning new converts to the faith, looking for a church to attend, are unaware of the dangers. They join a church family because the people in it are nice, warm, friendly people. But the leader may only be interested in the social aspect of church and is just 'tickling the ears' of the congregants.

In a church like that there is a lack of truth being preached, spiritually weak house groups and no space for the Holy Spirit to bring godly change in lives, no healing of spirit, soul or body, no equipping with the gifts of the Spirit, and no well-equipped and trained ministry team to help any new converts. Even the church's own members are trapped in the occult, sexual sin, pornography, gambling, addictions and a host of other demonic activities. How on earth are new Christians to be set free? Yet that's why Jesus came, to set the captives free.

Role of the Church

What then is the role of the local church? The church is not just a 'bless-me-club' or a place where you can come, sing a few songs, listen to messages which make you feel better but don't challenge you to do anything. What about putting God's Word firmly into people's hearts so it can consciously and deliberately bring change for the better? Did Jesus come to earth merely to save us for a trip to Heaven when we die? No, definitely not!

Why did Jesus appoint disciples? Was it just to establish church congregations around the world? I tell you the truth, Jesus came to establish His Church for us all to continue His work here on earth. As we read the four Gospels, Matthew, Mark, Luke and John, we learn about all the things Jesus did. And as He was doing all these amazing miracles, preaching the Good News, the people were believing in Him, putting their faith in Him and receiving Him as Lord of their lives.

Because they believed, people everywhere were being healed of sickness and disease, and many were set free from demonic intrusion. This is what Jesus trained His disciples to do, so that, after His death, they could carry on doing what He did. What we learn about the disciples of Jesus' day should apply to the Church today. Every Christian is part of the Church. God is speaking to every one of us.

Equipping in the Church

The disciples (which includes us) were needing to be properly equipped for astounding work nobody had ever seen before. For those who were following Jesus this work was to become an everyday occurrence. To do it, they needed the

Holy Spirit and the permission to operate in the power of God. They could not get enough of this new teaching which was being confirmed by the power of God. It made so much sense. In Christ Jesus they witnessed God on earth.

> *You know what has happened throughout Judea, beginning in Galilee after the baptism that John preached— how God anointed Jesus of Nazareth with the Holy Spirit and power, and how he went around doing good and healing all who were under the power of the devil, because God was with him. "We are witnesses of everything he did in the country of the Jews and in Jerusalem." (Acts10:37-39)*

The time eventually came when Jesus sent them out two by two to put into practice all they had learned. Jesus knew the time was ripe to finally give them authority and power to continue His work here on earth.

> *Calling the Twelve to him, he sent them out two by two and gave them authority over evil spirits. These were his (Jesus) instructions: "Take nothing for the journey except a staff—no bread, no bag, no money in your belts. Wear sandals but not an extra tunic. Whenever you enter a house, stay there until you leave that town. And if any place will not welcome you or listen to you, shake the dust off your feet when you leave, as a testimony against them." They went out and preached that people should repent. They drove out many demons and anointed many sick people with oil and healed them. (Mark 6:7-13)*

So they set out and went from village to village, preaching the gospel and healing people everywhere. (Luke 9:6)

This was the exciting beginning of the Church of Jesus Christ. Now that they had tasted and experienced for themselves what Jesus was teaching about and they had started demonstrating the power of God to everyone, it was a sign that He trusted them with God's power from on high.

What a responsibility on their shoulders to take the ministry of Jesus into all the world! Now, that same responsibility falls on our shoulders. Remember, before that, God was silent for four hundred years, and now, in their lifetime, God had sent His Son to teach twelve men, then the seventy-two, and then countless others around the globe. It was the day of small beginnings which we are told in Scripture not to despise.

Beware of the Dark Places

God is fair and just and does not seek to exercise control over anyone. That's not God's style at all. When He created us, He gave us the ability to make choices. Adam and Eve could choose whether to follow God's instruction to not eat the fruit of a tree in the middle of the garden. A simple instruction, yes, but it was important to God.

God knows everything going on in our heart and mind. We think nobody knows the things we do secretly, in the dark, behind closed doors when nobody's watching. Wrong! God's watching the good and the bad of all we do. When it's in line with His will for our lives, the consequence results in an appropriate blessing. When it's out of His will for our lives, He is obliged to step back, because we are choosing to do something He has warned us not to do: we are doing something that Satan wants us to do.

You can be assured Satan's way will never end well. Why? Because there are good consequences if we obey God' will and His instructions but bad consequences if we disobey or ignore God's instructions. Disobedience to God is called sin. There is no other appropriate word for sin. We effectively and voluntarily hand ourselves over to Satan for him to dish out a consequence. It can begin with recklessly taking one drug from a drug pusher and end up, at a later stage, being admitted to a psychiatric hospital.

I am not saying one sin is going to mean you will end up that way. When we continuously overstep the mark with God, however, we ourselves are giving rights to the enemy who is seeking to steal, kill and destroy. Give him a little finger, and he'll go for an arm.

Do not be deceived by the dangerous teaching about hyper-grace which is going around, and which says you can do whatever you want, and the grace of God will always cover you. God's grace certainly covers us, but only if we truly repent and turn from our sinful ways. God's grace does stretch a long way, but be careful not to make the mistake of presuming upon God's grace.

On the day you repent, God the Father, full of mercy, will be waiting for you to receive you back into the family. There might have to be a period of discipline that you have to go through, but that is because He loves you and He is treating you like a son or a daughter.

My son, do not make light of the Lord's discipline, and do not lose heart when he rebukes you, because the Lord disciplines the one he loves, and he chastens everyone he accepts as his son. Endure hardship as discipline; God is treating you as his children. For what children are not disciplined by their father? If you are not disciplined—and everyone undergoes discipline—then you are not legitimate, not true sons and daughters at all. (Hebrews 12:5-8)

Deception in the World

People in deception have targeted the Church of Jesus Christ for 2000 years. People who choose to say 'no' to following Christ, do so on their own soulish terms. Today they use the powerful media platform to intimidate and manipulate people, thus closing their spiritual eyes to God's truth. This can be used as a powerful weapon by the devil, who turns deception into hatred of those in the Church who disagree with them and object to their push to promote teachings that fly in the face of God.

The rise of secular Humanism and the ideologies it spawns are increasingly becoming a challenge to Christian believers. Secular Humanism basically teaches that there is no God and no absolute plumb line of truth. Each person can decide what is morally or ethically right and has the right to determine the shape and meaning of their own life. It promotes the idea that we all have a right to choose our gender and a right to express our sexuality in the way we choose, and others have to respect our choices, without question.

*'See to it that no one takes you captive through
hollow and deceptive philosophy, which depends on
human tradition and the elemental spiritual forces
of this world rather than on Christ.' (Colossians 2:8)*

These ideas, often referred to as 'The New Normal', have been enshrined into law in many countries. Activists supporting these ideas are continually pressuring governments that their ideologies must be taught in schools. They claim that anyone who opposes their ideas is being offensive and discriminatory towards them, and they are pressuring governments to introduce legislation to criminalize any such opposition.

For instance, marriage of one man to one woman, as God intended, is being challenged by introducing a New Normal for marriage. The intention is to condition the minds of Christians and straight-thinking people to a place where, eventually, everyone will agree and say, "It's okay to change God's law and make a new man-made law. People must now be free to choose any partner, regardless of whatever sex they are. We will also make it a criminal offence for anyone to disagree and say that, in their opinion, this law is wrong."

Another example of new laws coming which want to turn our children away from God, is allowing them to decide what sex they would like to be, irrespective of what sex God created them to be. And even more devastating, laws are in place, not allowing their parents to have any say in the matter, under penalty of having their children removed from their care and placed into foster care. This is the New Normal! Many more examples could be cited. Do we as the Church agree with this? Where are our voices?

Church Leaders in Deception

It is also horrifying to hear of church leaders around the world agreeing to this New Normal and positioning themselves under the world's ways by adding their stamp of approval on what is fast becoming politically correct. They agree with the New Normal which is actually saying, "The views and the wishes of society are more important than the ways of God our Creator'.

Please hear me, I am not against the Church per se; I am not the judge. I am, however, prepared to say that much of where the world is leading is wrong. In any case, why is the world leading the Church? We need to bear in mind that God is not politically correct. God is truth.

Imagine the scenario where people might say to the engineers of a car manufacturer, "I'm not going to put petrol or diesel in the tank as your instructions insist I should. Instead, I'm going to use water and sugar and, if you don't honor the warranty, I will take you to court. On top of that, I'm going to inflate the tires to half the recommended pressure, and you had better fall in line with the way I think. Your manufacturer's handbook for proper care of this vehicle no longer applies. I'm introducing a New Normal for this vehicle and I'm making a law which says, if you don't agree, you are liable for a hefty fine or imprisonment or both."

The manufacturer would have no more say in how people should maintain and take care of their car, because the masses, who have come into wicked agreement with each other, have decided they know better. Would the manufacturer agree with those terms? Then why should God, as the 'Manufacturer' of each and every human being, agree with those wishing to change His instructions? He loves each one He has created. It is up to each one of us to accept His love or reject it.

I know that is a rather ridiculous scenario, but I feel it's applicable to what's happening in the world today. There are those, under the guidance of Satan, rebelling, as Satan did, against God's creation of what is good and healthy for our lives here on earth.

Those who choose to follow Christ as their redeemer have got choices to make. Believers have to ask themselves, "Do I follow the truth of the Bible or the fine-sounding arguments of those who proclaim half-truth?" What is happening, however, is causing many to go astray, and causing further division in an already divided Church.

On the other hand, and this is becoming increasingly clear, activists are afraid of the rising up of the true, uncompromising Church. That's why they are now trying to persuade governments to make laws which would effectively silence the voice of Bible-believing Christians. This reminds me of the story of Shadrach, Meshach and Abednego in Daniel, Chapter 3. They were persecuted for refusing to bow down to the golden image set up by King Nebuchadnezzar. Let it be clear that God will never be silenced.

Keep Your Spiritual Eyes Open

What we see happening around us and the increasing intensity in the battle should not surprise us. The Word of God tells us a lot about what is going to happen before the return of Jesus. Do not remain ignorant about these happenings. Do not close your spiritual eyes. Watch the weather patterns, droughts, floods, volcanoes and the changing climate.

Take note of what's happening in politics, the Middle East, America, China, North Korea, the United Kingdom and Europe. Look at the aggressive advancement of ideologies based on secular Humanism and the New Normal, undermining Christian beliefs and values. These are all signs of what is written in days of old and recorded in the Bible.

Jesus answered: "Watch out that no one deceives you. For many will come in my name, claiming, 'I am the Christ,' and will deceive many. You will hear of wars and rumors of wars, but see to it that you are not alarmed. Such things must happen, but the end is still to come. Nation will rise against nation, and kingdom against kingdom. There will be famines and earthquakes in various places. All these are the beginning of birth pains. Then you will be handed over to be persecuted and put to death, and you will be hated by all nations because of me. At that time many will turn away from the faith and will betray and hate each other, and many false prophets will appear and deceive many people. Because of the increase of wickedness, the love of most will grow cold, but he who stands firm to the end will be saved" (Matthew 24:4-13)

For false Christs and false prophets will appear and perform great signs and miracles to deceive even the elect—if that were possible. See, I have told you ahead of time. (Matthew 24:24-25)

God Exposing Deception

However, I believe God is allowing those with unscrupulous ideas based on the New Normal to present their views at this time to test each Christian's heart. Each individual Christian is having to look at whether they believe God's truth or the world's ideas. Let me be clear that, as a Christian I love all people, no matter what they have done, but I cannot accept any of their wrong practices which are out of line with God's will. I also believe it is God's heart to restore each one of us to His truth.

> *When the Son of Man comes in his glory, and all the angels with him, he will sit on his throne in heavenly glory. All the nations will be gathered before him, and he will separate the people one from another as a shepherd separates the sheep from the goats. (Matthew 25:31-32)*

Should you find yourself moving away from God's instruction for life, it is never too late to humble yourself before God and make your paths straight in Jesus' name. It does not matter which denomination we belong to, but it does matter whether we are right in our hearts before God.

> *My eyes are on all their ways; they are not hidden from me, nor is their sin concealed from my eyes. (Jeremiah 16:17)*

> *"if my people, who are called by my name, will humble themselves and pray and seek my face and turn from their wicked ways, then will I hear from heaven and will forgive their sin and will heal their land." (2 Chronicles 7:14)*

My Prayer About deception

My prayer is that readers will read this book, asking God to give them discernment. Then He will help open blinded spiritual eyes. The Deceiver is using every means of twisted truth to turn the minds and thoughts of people away from God's ways and to develop an ungodly view of human rights and a New Normal of political or denominational correctness in the place of God's will and His way. Despite his many different strategies, knowing and believing the truth will reveal his deception.

> *"my people are destroyed from lack of knowledge."*
> *(Hosea 4:6)*

The following is a very important scripture to take note of. Let us pray for eyes to be opened that they may see the light and be saved.

> *Rather, we have renounced secret and shameful ways; we do not use deception, nor do we distort the word of God. On the contrary, by setting forth the truth plainly we commend ourselves to every man's conscience in the sight of God. And even if our gospel is veiled, it is veiled to those who are perishing. The god of this age has blinded the minds of unbelievers, so that they cannot see the light of the gospel of the glory of Christ, who is the image of God. (2 Corinthians 4:2-4)*

The Spirit of understanding we need is beautifully expressed in this passage of Scripture in Isaiah Chapter 11.

> *A shoot will come up from the stump of Jesse; from his roots a Branch will bear fruit. The Spirit of the*

LORD will rest on him—the Spirit of wisdom and of understanding, the Spirit of counsel and of power, the Spirit of knowledge and of the fear of the LORD— and he will delight in the fear of the LORD. (Isaiah 11:1-3)

In this chapter we have been looking at how the father of lies introduces deception into the world and into the Church in order to close our eyes to God's revealed truth. In the next chapter we will remind ourselves to be vigilant in dealing with temptation and our thinking, so that we can live in the light and walk in victory.

Chapter 9
The Road to Victory

When we become believers, our eyes are spiritually open to receive God's truth into our lives. We see the Bible in a new light. Scriptures, even those we are familiar with, seem full of new understanding and relevance to our life. The enemy of our souls sees what has happened and we now become one of his targets.

With our eyes open, we see more clearly the nature of the battle. Although still living in the world, we have been given spiritual weapons such as forgiveness, repentance, praise and worship to deploy against the enemy and make sure he is unable to close our eyes again to God's truth.

> "...though we live in the world, we do not wage war as the world does. The weapons we fight with are not the weapons of the world. On the contrary, they have divine power to demolish strongholds." (2 Corinthians 10:3-4)

The Conflict Within Us

There is a conflict within us, a spiritual tug-of-war. The Holy Spirit wants us to do God's will, and the sinful nature within us entices us to do Satan's evil deeds. Sometimes there is an opposing evil spirit at work in the person at the same time. We subconsciously make decisions all day long. They may be a mixture of good and bad, right and wrong. As we grow in Christ and renew our mind day by day, we begin to lean more and more to the side of righteousness and God's blessing to help others and to do good. Paul in his letter to the Ephesians gives us this encouraging advice:

So I say, live by the Spirit, and you will not gratify the desires of the sinful nature. For the sinful nature desires what is contrary to the Spirit, and the Spirit what is contrary to the sinful nature. They are in conflict with each other, so that you do not do what you want. But if you are led by the Spirit, you are not under law. (Galatians 5:16-18)

The prince of this world is always, and when I say always, I mean always, at work looking for that weak link in our armor to sneak in to whisper in our ear to disobey God.

This is because all of mankind is created in the image of God and therefore loved by God. God may hate what we're doing, but He loves us so much. Satan hates the spiritual image and likeness in us, because looking at us reminds him of God.

What then is the role of the Church? I'm talking about you and me. The answer is to earnestly pray, snatch lives from the fire, make effective disciples and fight the good fight for what is right, fair and just in God's eyes. When Satan tempted Jesus in the desert with promises of power and worldly wealth, Jesus rebuked him and fought him off with Scripture saying, *"Away from me Satan! For it is written: 'Worship the Lord your God and serve Him only'"* (Matthew 4:10). What Satan wants for our lives is opposite to that which God wants for our lives. As we live in the world, we must be careful not to fall in love with what the world has to offer.

Do not love the world or anything in the world. If anyone loves the world, the love of the Father is not in him. For everything in the world—the cravings of sinful man, the lust of his eyes and the boasting of what he has and does—comes not from the Father but from the world. The world and its desires pass away, but the man who does the will of God lives forever. (1 John 2:15-17)

The rulers, the authorities and the powers of this dark world, those not under the rule of God the Father, as well as spiritual forces of evil in the heavenly realms, are influencing people on earth to do their will.

Gratifying the flesh seems to be the major attraction in all sorts of ways to draw people away from the amazing life of holiness in Christ Jesus. Satan and his followers want to keep Christians in darkness. He wants them, through unhealed ungodly lifestyles, attitudes and behavior to destroy their testimony, making them ineffective and less powerful witnesses of Christ.

Whom Do We Obey

The devil is prowling around, seeking whom he may devour (1 Peter 5:8). He manipulates in order to trick and tempt us into doing something his way rather than God's way. That's why he has to prowl around, because he has no hold on Christians who are following God and are doing no evil.

Satan's objective is to subtly kill, steal and destroy us. Both Jesus and Satan are looking for our obedience. When we are disobedient to God, we are walking in Satan's territory, and he wants to keep us there long enough to wrap us up in some bondage or another.

The devil offers lies and empty promises, sometimes with a dash of truth mixed in, just enough to raise our hopes so we think we're on the right track. He might give just one sentence which sounds good. He will offer anything, just to get you to say "yes" to him and not to Jesus.

Satan's offer, however good it sounds, will eventually lead to the depths of his domain, which is hell and destruction. Jesus' way will always lead to inner peace, joy and everlasting life. It's a no-brainer. All Satan wanted was for Jesus to be subservient to him. But Jesus knew the tricks of this rogue, and He also knew the love of His Father and trusted His every word.

Jesus, while He was on earth, like every one of us, faced tests throughout His life to show us all the way of obedience. Keep your eyes and ears open to the cunning teachings of wolves in sheep's clothing. They want you to throw caution to the wind just for one small taste of what the world has to offer, like a fly fisherman, who deceives fish with an artificial fly in which a hook is embedded.

God Does Not Tempt

God knows how we will respond to tests but we don't, until they challenge us. Is that fair of God, to test us? God does not tempt us, but He does allow tests, just as a school gives tests to students to prove they can be promoted to the next level.

> *When tempted, no one should say, "God is tempting me." For God cannot be tempted by evil, nor does he tempt anyone; but each one is tempted when, by his own evil desire, he is dragged away and enticed (James 1:13-14)*

Satan Tempts Jesus

The scene of Satan tempting Jesus is similar to the scene in the Garden of Eden where this same devil tempted Eve. God was disappointed with Adam, because he listened to Eve and not to God the Father, who had clearly told him not to eat the fruit of that particular tree.

We all have our own private scenes like the one in the garden. We all have to face that moment of asking ourselves, "Do I"? or "Don't I?" We face these tests on a daily basis, because the devil and his demons are bombarding us all the time to think, do and say wrong things, and every moment we are faced with making godly or ungodly decisions, just as Adam and Eve had to do.

How strange it is that in church sermons, one rarely hears of warnings of the dark world trying to extinguish the light of a Christian's voice, testimony and reputation through sin! But once we understand the tactics of the enemy of our souls, we can much more easily recognize what's happing spiritually in our daily walk.

I explained earlier the 'born again' process, when Jesus comes in by His Holy Spirit and He makes us new. At that moment, our spirit becomes alive to Christ. Before that, we were in Satan's territory, he was our father, we were his subjects and we listened to his voice. Our spiritual eyes were closed to God and our spirits were deaf to God.

Now that we are born again by the Spirit of God our eyes are open to God. We can choose to resist the temptation and go God's way. An individual's inability to gain victory over a particular temptation would indicate the need for inner healing of their emotions and human spirit and perhaps a measure of deliverance.

> *No temptation has overtaken you except what is common to mankind. And God is faithful; he will not let you be tempted beyond what you can bear. But when you are tempted, he will also provide a way out so that you can endure it. (1 Corinthians 10:13)*

When Leaders Fall

We need to keep our eyes open and be aware of the enemy's strategy to tempt us and cause us to fall. Pastors and leaders are also subject to temptation, so what do you do if they fail? We need to remember that they are only human, and they are subject to the same temptations, perhaps even more so, as Christians who are not called to lead.

The truth is, you don't really know what's happening in their private life and whether any part of it is not true to the plumb line of God. You can't look at the splinter in someone else's eye and ignore the plank in your own eye. We may be addressing leaders here, but the same principle applies to each one of us.

If your pastor or leader falls from grace, or compromises his belief in the Scriptures, you will find there are immature and undiscerning Christians who will follow him, but the mature, discerning and uncompromising Christian will really struggle to receive anything further from him. You may be deeply hurt, so deeply that you lose trust in all Christian leaders and even the Church. You may even blame God for what has happened to the leader you so respected.

If this is where you are, it is best to go before God and forgive the leader and all those who sided with his ungodly view. As disappointed as you may be, do not discard them. If given the opportunity, encourage them to acknowledge their fault, to repent, to ask for forgiveness and in humility to submit to godly discipline (Hebrews 12:4-12), as this is God's way of restoring His children. Please pray for your leaders, as they are as vulnerable as any other Christian.

Through a lack of understanding of the enemy's tactics, when something bad happens to a good leader, offended people leave the church in their droves. This is the 'follow my leader' phenomenon. Sometimes people follow so blindly that they get hurt in the process and fall into the danger of losing their faith. As a result of deep disappointment in a leader, many immature Christians have turned away from the Church and even from God.

We should follow God, not a human leader. The mistake many make is joining a church because of a likable leader. I know it does help, but that should not be our reason for joining. If God led you to that church, it is not because of the leaders, but because God has a purpose for you there. Should a leader fall, are you going to say it's God's fault He led you there? However, an unrepentant leader is a different situation altogether. I would rather stick with a leader who is genuinely repentant than one who is brash, prideful and unrepentant, no matter how close a friend they may be. And I say this kindly.

Do we see ourselves better than any leader? No, I'm sure we don't. We need to come alongside and assist in every way we can to seek God's face for the restoration of our leaders, and for that matter, any Christian who has made a mistake. Fallen leaders will always need to be lovingly supported and cared for. Yes, appropriate discipline needs to be applied and they need to be taken out of all ministry functions.

But if leaders refuse to confess their error, to repent and ask for forgiveness, and refuse to submit themselves to ministry for restoration, that is the time for you to consider finding a new spiritual home that is safe. Should it ever get to that point, as I have seen in many cases, it will not go well with unrepentant leaders. God will deal with them in His own good time, and hopefully they will allow themselves to be wooed back by God's love and grace to full restoration.

Find a Safe Place to Fall

There is nothing hidden from God's eyes. He sees and knows every single thing we say, do or think. It's better to stay clean before God. If you are currently in the place where you are not doing right in God's eyes, He sees it. If you have messed up in the past, it's best to find someone you can really trust, confess it, repent of it, ask God for forgiveness and make good decisions from now on. Maybe it would be good to forgive yourself for the wrongs you have committed.

> *Therefore confess your sins to each other and pray for each other so that you may be healed. The prayer of a righteous man is powerful and effective. (James 5:16)*

The point I want to make here is that, if you are a pastor and want to make right with God, do you feel free to confess your sin to a colleague? It would be unwise for a leader to confide in a member of the congregation. If not a colleague, then find someone safe outside of your circle. If you are a church member, do you feel free to confess to your pastor or to a ministry team person?

If you are a Christian who is not in a church fellowship because of past issues with church leadership, and you have something you want to get off your chest and make right with God, would you go to a local church in your area for ministry? The answer would probably be no. So where can you go? It's a shame really, but it's something that can be changed. The Church should be a safe place to confess our sins and walk the road of restoration.

In the healing ministry my wife and I established here in Pretoria, we know the dilemma many people have when it comes to issues like this. They see the church as not being a safe place to make right with God. They give various reasons, but the most common are, "I will be judged", "They don't respect confidentiality", "I get looked down upon", "They don't listen to my heart but are quick to brush me off with rushed prayer", "I feel as if they are doing me a favor by giving me their time", "I feel worse after ministry, and I should never have gone in the first place", "They don't understand my brokenness", and "I don't trust them".

Of course, the same issues and comments can arise in our ministry, and they do from time to time. But, on the whole, they don't, because we understand and love broken people. We understand the importance of confidentiality and the damage it can cause if it is broken, not just for the sake of the person coming for help but also for our own reputation as a ministry. We understand the power of welcoming a hurting person and making them feel special and cared for.

We understand the power of quality time. Our appointments are either for a morning or afternoon, a full day, or even a week. The church needs to care for broken people. Restoring broken lives is time consuming I know, but our investment in caring for God's sheep is priceless. Raise up and properly equip an effective ministry team in your church to help care for the flock and the community in your area.

The Battle for the Mind

Do not conform any longer to the pattern of this world, but be transformed by the renewing of your mind. Then you will be able to test and approve what God's will is—his good, pleasing and perfect will. (Romans 12:2)

The mind is a major battle ground for all believers. Satan would love for us to fill our minds with lies about God, about ourselves and about others. The enemy of our souls bombards Christian minds with lies such as: 'You are a failure', 'You can't trust anyone', 'God does not really love and care for you' or 'You are not valuable or precious'.

Romans 12:1-2 encourages us not to be a conformist to the pattern of this world, but to conform and live life the way God intended us to live – to please Him. In the first verse, Paul includes not only our minds, but also our bodies. They are to be holy and pleasing to God. Coming out of the worldly way of living which was not always pleasing to God sometimes needs much help from a more mature believer.

When God tells us not to conform to the pattern of this world, I think He knows what the awful consequences are if we do. After all, He is our Creator and knows exactly how our minds and bodies should function and the lifestyle we need to live. He knows what pleases Him and how to help us get the best out of life on earth.

He also knows what the devil is looking for. He looks for any gap, any kink in our armor that may be a sign of weakness or a character flaw. He will work on the weak area until we allow him in, just a little. He is, however, not interested in just one little weak spot in us, as he wants to control our whole being until we are destroyed. That's the only way he can keep us out of his way. Otherwise, should he allow us to grow spiritually strong and become mature, we are his biggest threat.

> *I can do everything through him who gives me strength. (Philippians 4:13)*

Paul understood the nature of the battle in the mind and how the enemy would try to deceive us to believe things that are not true. He tells us that we need to test all our thoughts and take them captive. If our thoughts are not in line with what the Bible says or if our thoughts are not in agreement with what Jesus says, we should take them captive and not allow ourselves to be controlled by them.

> *We demolish arguments and every pretension that sets itself up against the knowledge of God, and we take captive every thought to make it obedient to Christ. (2 Corinthians 10:5)*

Sharon's Testimony

Sharon's testimony describes how the enemy can use wrong beliefs to hold us in fear and captivity.

'I grew up in a family that loved and served God. I asked Jesus to be my Lord and Savior when I was a little girl of eight years old. When I was thirteen, I suddenly found myself in a spiritual battle that I was not ready for. I found myself inexplicably terrified of being alone and in the dark. At night, I would find myself aware of something evil in my bedroom and so I became afraid to sleep. I had to have a nightlight in my bedroom for months.

I became afraid to be on my own at home and even as a young married woman, would not go out of the back door alone at night. I still had a constant feeling of being intimidated in my spirit. Sometimes it even felt as though something was trying to claw its way out of me which was very scary.

What if, as a believer in Christ, I was actually demonized? What if, instead of receiving the Holy Spirit, I had received 'another spirit'? These questions plagued me constantly and put me into a state of fear and confusion, even about my salvation. I was too afraid to share with anyone else what I was thinking and feeling. I became terrified of the demonic. The enemy was building a stronghold of lies in my mind. I had begun to believe that the enemy had more power over my life than God.

But God had not forgotten me. Attending courses at Ellel reminded me of my identity in Christ and all that Jesus had done for me on the cross. I also realised that I had fallen into the traps of the enemy which began to be revealed as I believed the truth. I gradually brought my many fears to the Lord, repented of my unbelief and re-established the Lordship of Jesus over my life. I received prayer ministry and deliverance, and the chains of bondage began to fall away.

I also realised that I needed to stand in what the Lord had done for me and in the authority that He won for me at such a great cost. Whenever those feelings of terror, which had abated, tried to return I was armed. I would cry out to the Lord, and He would give me verses of Scripture that I would cling on to for dear life.

As I stood on the Word and trusted the Lord to deliver me, the episodes became shorter and eventually disappeared altogether. Today, as a prayer minister, I am able to encourage and help others to use the authority given in Jesus' name to deal with demonic strongholds over their lives.'

I have known Sharon for many years and the above testimony of the change in her life is amazing. It illustrates how the enemy does not want us to reach our full potential. Once we understand who we are in Christ Jesus and receive the correct discipleship and training, we are a threat to the enemy and can fulfil God's plans and purpose for our life.

Finding Our Purpose

At a young age, we need help to navigate life on paths that lead to grace, goodness and kindness. Unfortunately, many of the guardians we have had, were themselves abused and misdirected in life. As a result, we may not have received the guidance and nurture we needed, and our spirit may have been damaged.

Our journey through life can be likened to a bird with a damaged wing desperately trying to soar with the eagles and trying to find the right way. We will struggle to reach our full potential and the way we live life will be based on our past experiences. Often, we try to find the meaning and purpose of life in our own strength. However, life's true purpose, which God has planned for every individual on earth, can only be found in Him.

> *For we are God's handiwork, created in Christ Jesus to do good works, which God prepared in advance for us to do. (Ephesians 2:10)*

Some find God's purpose earlier than others. Others have their own ideas of what they want to do with their lives, not to say that's necessarily wrong, but when we know we're in God's plan, it is just so fulfilling. I only found God's real purpose for my life at the age of fifty-eight. From then until now have been the best years of my life. Reaching God's purpose is achieving God's effectiveness for our life. If we seek God's plan, He will give us understanding.

> *We know also that the Son of God has come and has given us understanding, so that we may know him who is true. And we are in him who is true—even in his Son Jesus Christ. He is the true God and eternal life. (1 John 5:20)*

To prevent giving the enemy a foothold in our lives, an intimate relationship and knowing the One holding the plumb line of truth is so important in discerning what is true and what is false. As we do this, we can live in the Kingdom of God with our eyes open and not closed.

Chapter 10
With Open Eyes

*But seek first his kingdom and his righteousness,
and all these things will be given to you as well.
(Matthew 6:33)*

This is the first scripture given to me by my friends, Jan and
Pam Robbertze, after I received Jesus as Lord. It has really
become my heart, and I often quote it. Seeking first His
kingdom and his righteousness is where it all starts and
should become a continuous lifestyle.

The impact on me of the fact that Jesus would save a wretch
like me was huge. The fact that God would trust me was so
humbling. When He answered my prayer to be filled with His
Holy Spirit, I realised how His love for me was so genuine.
Me of all people! It was with that confidence in Christ that I
immediately developed a heart for evangelism and praying
for the sick.

I regard our salvation, the immediate translation from the
kingdom of darkness into the Kingdom of God, as being the
first step to our healing. Salvation for the Christian means
'deliverance or rescue from evil'. It is in the Kingdom of God
that real life with God begins. I needed to be discipled and
equipped to know God's heart for me and for others.

Knowing God More

God spoke to me even last year and told me in the early hours
of the morning, that *the more I knew Him, the more I would
know myself.* That for me is awesome! For so many years of
my life I have had a sense of unworthiness, rejection and

failure. Whenever I have an opportunity to preach or teach, these topics are often raised in the question time. This makes me realise what a huge problem they are in the Church. I've had healing in all three of these areas, but what about those people in the Church who haven't?

I had, and still have, a deep concern for people attending church, as well as those not attending church, who are still trapped in the kingdom of darkness. The extraordinary thing that Beryl and I realised is that, before we received Jesus as Lord, while still in our unsaved state, we both had a heart for hurting and broken people.

Our desire to help others in their healing started off with the journey of receiving our own healing. When we start learning how to help others, so much triggers into our own lives. It sort of pops up to the surface from deep within and presents itself for attention. God is just so gentle with us. It's as if the closer we draw to God, the more we allow Him to deal with us.

Come near to God and he will come near to you.
James 4:8(a)

But there is a condition. The verse goes on to say:

Wash your hands, you sinners, and purify your hearts, you double-minded. (James 4:8b)

Healing cannot take place with all the infection inside a wound lying under the surface of a scab. The Holy Spirit comes and gently helps us remove the scab and cleanse the wound. It is so freeing, and the sense of cleansing is felt deep within us.

Ministering in the power of the Holy Spirit is incredible. Even when praying over the phone, we experienced many thousands of salvations and recommitments, supernatural healings, and God's provision for those in need.

Our ministry to the Lord is always two-fold. It is firstly reaching out to the lost who are still in Satan's kingdom, and, secondly, ministering to the hurting people in God's Kingdom.

Have You been Deceived?

In Chapter one I shared how Beryl and I were ministering in Pretoria when the apartheid system started falling away after 1994 and the new ANC government was established. At that time, *'Truth and Reconciliation'*, which was a court restorative justice system, was established. This allowed people to tell their stories so as to get some form of closure for lost loved ones and for the perpetrators of human rights violations to say sorry and ask for forgiveness.

It was only when the shocking stories of these violations became public that the white population realised how they had been lied to and misled. As black people joined the congregation, I can't tell you how many times I asked for forgiveness for myself and on behalf of all white folk for allowing ourselves to be 'conveniently' deceived.

We had been deceived into believing the lie that apartheid was the only way to avoid a communist take-over of South Africa. We believed the lie that there was even scriptural support to justify the government's policy. Our eyes had become blinded to the truth and the needless suffering, hurt and pain that resulted.

Let's bring this into the context of this book. I believed and allowed an ungodly government to lie to me, and through fear I closed my eyes to the truth of the situation. But as soon as my spiritual eyes were opened, I was able to take corrective action. I have repented over and over again to many people for my lack of discernment. How gracious every black person has been to grant their forgiveness.

The lesson I have learnt is that there is good and bad in every political party, and I believe this applies equally to church organisations. Sometimes we have to check our hearts asking, "Is my heart in line with God's heart?" We need to check what is being said against the plumb line of God's truth. We need to ask ourselves, "Have I been passive and just accepted what I have been told? Have I allowed myself to be deceived and missed God's plans and purposes for my life?"

Follow the Manufacturer's Instructions

This book is not about what the world is doing or not doing or whatever New Normal they want to establish. This book is a call to return to God's normal and to follow the original Manufacturer's instructions. It is a call to examine whether our practices and beliefs are actually in accord with God's truth and the instructions given to us by Jesus.

Some will choose to believe the words of the Manufacturer - God the Creator. Others will continue to 'put water and sugar in their fuel tank of life'. Those who believe the Manufacturer is speaking truth, have the opportunity to change their old habits and ways and begin afresh by filling their hearts and minds with the original truth of God's will and His way. As they do this, they will discover that life on earth becomes considerably more fulfilling.

Inflating our 'tyres' to the correct pressure, as specified by the Manufacturer, will go a long way in helping us to navigate the journey of life. Living life God's way certainly helps us to find meaning to life, direction, hope, purpose, love, peace and joy, even on the rough road towards life's end.

It may be time for the Church of Jesus to remove the 'sugar from their tank', check the level of 'holy oil' and put the correct pressure in their 'tyres' to follow God's truth. This will allow the power of the Holy Spirit to once again fill our sanctuaries and watch over our going out and coming in (Psalm 121:8).

Listening to and following the Manufacturer's instructions, the Holy Bible, will stop the enemy closing our eyes to the truth and will enable us to move into God's destiny for our life with our eyes fully open.

And Finally

'Father God, I thank You that You opened my eyes to the truth. I pray that You will show any reader of this book whether their eyes have been blinded to Your truth, or their understanding blurred in any way. Please give them the boldness and courage to address any such issues. I pray that their spiritual eyes may always be fully open and that their life and ministry will be completely in accord with Your destiny for their life. Amen.'

About the Author

Born in Johannesburg, South Africa, in 1942 but raised in Port Elizabeth, Derek became a managing company director in the business world. Whilst working in Namibia he met and married Beryl. They have been married for more than fifty years and have two wonderful children and five beautiful grandchildren.

In Namibia Derek and Beryl pioneered Life Line - a non-profit secular telephone counselling service. After becoming Christians, they used this experience to establish Telefriend, a Christian telephone helpline in South Africa.

Called to full time Christian work, Derek spent twelve years in pastoral ministry, with Beryl alongside, in a large church in Pretoria. They have always had a special interest in helping hurting and broken people and a desire to see them restored and equipped.

When they discovered that Ellel Ministries had a similar vision and experience in this area, they sensed a strong call of God to change the direction of their lives. They hence made the huge step of leaving their church and spending two years in the UK, being equipped and receiving healing ministry for themselves.

Since their return to South Africa in 2001, they have been pioneering and establishing Ellel Ministries in Africa, including Shere House in Pretoria and centres in KwaZulu Natal, Rwanda and Kenya. All these centres offer help and training to Christians who are earnestly seeking healing and all that God has for them.

Derek and Beryl understand the challenges and struggles faced by pastors and leaders. They have a heart to encourage them and see them healed and free of any bondages that would prevent them being effective in their service for the King of kings.

Recommended Reading

These books will help you to understand the healing Ministry of Jesus.

'Healing Through Deliverance' (The Foundation and Practice of Deliverance Ministry) by Peter Horrobin ISBN 9781852408664

'Soul Ties' (The Unseen Bond in Relationships) by David Cross   ISBN9781852404512

'Trapped by Control' (How to Find Freedom) by David Cross   ISBN9781852405014

'Healing from the Consequences of Accident, Shock and Trauma' by Peter Horrobin ISBN9781852407438

'Rescued from Rejection' (Finding Security in God's Loving Acceptance) by Denise Cross ISBN9781852405380

'Hope and Healing for the Abused' by Paul and Liz Griffin   ISBN9781852404802

'Anger – How Do You Handle it?' by Paul and Liz Griffin   ISBN9781852404505

'Stepping Stones to the Father Heart of God' by Margaret Silvester   ISBN9781852406233

'The Choice' (Serving Heaven or Serving Hell) by Andy Robertson   ISBN9781852407117

'Sarah' (From an abusive childhood and the depths of suicidal despair to a life of hope and freedom) by Sarah Shaw   ISBN9781852405113

'Lynda, From Accident & Trauma to Healing & Wholeness' by Lynda Scott   ISBN9781852408138

'The Dangers of Alternative Ways to Healing' (How to Avoid New Age Deception) by John Berry & David Cross   ISBN9781852405373

'God's Covering' (A Place of Healing) by David Cross   ISBN9781852404857

'Intercession and Healing' (Breaking Through with God) by Fiona Horrobin ISBN9781852405007

'Healing the Human Spirit' by Ruth Hawkey ISBN: 9781852408763

'God's Way Out of Depression' by David Cross ISBN9781852408091

'Discover Healing and Freedom' (Knowing and Living the Truth that Sets you Free) by Peter Horrobin   ISBN9781852408473

'Healing through Creativity' (A Bridge from the Head to the Heart - How Simple Creativity Can Bring Deep Healing from our Creator) by Fiona Horrobin ISBN9781852408374